The Narrow Path

Roy Flint

WESTBOW
PRESS
A DIVISION OF THOMAS NELSON

WestBow Press books may be ordered through booksellers or by contacting:

WestBow Press
A Division of Thomas Nelson
1663 Liberty Drive
Bloomington, IN 47403
www.westbowpress.com
1-(866) 928-1240

Because of the dynamic nature of the Internet, any Web addresses or links contained in this book may have changed since publication and may no longer be valid. The views expressed in this work are solely those of the author and do not necessarily reflect the views of the publisher, and the publisher hereby disclaims any responsibility for them.

Any people depicted in stock imagery provided by Thinkstock are models, and such images are being used for illustrative purposes only.

Certain stock imagery © Thinkstock.

ISBN: 978-1-4497-1041-5 (sc)
ISBN: 978-1-4497-1040-8 (e)

Library of Congress Control Number: 2010942658

Printed in the United States of America

WestBow Press rev. date: 4/14/2011

Dedication

This book is dedicated to my wife and family.

The words of Jesus Christ

"Enter by the narrow gate; for the gate is wide, and the way is broad that leads to destruction, and many are those who enter by it. For the gate is small and the way is narrow that leads to life, and few are those who find it" (Matthew 7:13–14, NIV).

Preface

This guide is put together to help with the discipleship of believers. Today, there are many great Christian books available in our stores for reading, but there seems to be a lack of foundational training or equipping information for believers, especially new ones, to use.

Many new believers today are not learning the foundational tenets of faith we as Christians should know. This may result in inconsistencies of worship, personal devotion, and ministry involvement. Many people in the church or outside it think they are right with God but are not. They have been led astray by false doctrine and deceived. They do not love God as they should and fail to see His true Holiness. They live a life of easy believe-ism and lukewarmness. In most cases it is because they lack knowledge about God. They don't know what His word says. They may have simply not been discipled correctly.

It is my desire to help disciple believers through this guide so that they will truly love God and walk with Him. Discipled people know who they are in Christ. They follow God through any circumstance.

"If you hold to My teaching you are really My disciples. Then you will know the truth and the truth will set you free" (John 8:31b–32, NIV).

A true believer is a true disciple. A true disciple will know the truth. Jesus also said in Matthew 28:19–20 for us to make disciples of all nations, baptizing them in the name of the Father, Son, and Holy Spirit. We are to teach them to obey all that Jesus commanded. Jesus is saying teach them about Me, who I AM, and how much I love them. I want them to know the truth and how they can live by the Spirit's power.

Discipleship is difficult, and following Jesus is costly. Today we want Jesus but not what He asks of us. We hope that part of it will just disappear. Yet, He wants us to understand what is asked of us and wants us to live our lives that way.

In Matthew 7:13–14, Jesus says, *"Enter through the narrow gate. For wide is the gate and broad is the road that leads to destruction, and many enter through it. But small is the gate and narrow the road that leads to life and only a few find it* (NIV).

The Christian life goes against the grain of this world. Yet it is the only way—through Christ and the cross. The narrow path has intersections with the tempter playing traffic cop at each one. To take one of these roads is to go down a dead end. The narrow path is the one Jesus told us to take. He asks us to deny ourselves and take up our cross in Mark 8:34–35. We, as believers, should lose our life to save it. We should be able to say that all we are and have is the Lord's. This is the growth process we need to be on. This is the road less traveled, the narrow path. It requires wisdom, but it is the only path for the redeemed.

Acknowledgments

I thank God for the privilege of knowing and serving Him. May this guide glorify Him. My prayer is that God uses this guide to bring many into His kingdom and help them grow. I thank my wife for her support and guidance in helping me put this guide together. I thank my parents for their prayers and support. Their encouragement helps keep me going. Many thanks to Senior Pastor Galen Greenwalt of the Vision Plus Church for his help. I thank Lionel Adams and other friends involved in reviewing this book for all their support. Your help was greatly appreciated. God bless you all.

What You Need as You Work through this Book

You will need a Bible, a pen or pencil, and a highlighter as you study. Take your time as you go through the book. It is not to be done quickly. Pray for the Holy Spirit to guide you every time you study this book and open your Bible. You may want to study it with other people. That can be done and is encouraged. You can study this book by yourself or with two or more people. Be sure to look up and read all the Scriptures that are not printed out. There are spaces for you to answer questions, and if you are unsure, the answers are in the back of the book. After you have finished the book, find others to share it with as you help guide them through it. May God bless you with spiritual growth as you spend time with Him.

Contents

Chapter 1

Do You Have Eternal Life with God?

This discipleship guide contains truths about the Christian walk. It is written for Christians and non-Christians alike. But for these truths to be better understood, a person should be as Jesus said to Nicodemus, "born again." Jesus told Nicodemus that he must be born again to enter the kingdom of God (John 3:3–5). So it is the same for every person who wishes to enter the kingdom. A person needs salvation. Salvation simply means deliverance from danger. The danger is a lack of knowing God. Not seeing God work in your life. Not living eternally with God and having the joy of Jesus as your Savior and Lord. The result is God's judgment and eternal damnation after death.

Are you born again? To be born again, three things must happen to a person. The first comes by believing the Word of God. In John 3:5–8, Jesus said, *"Most assuredly I say to you, unless one is born of water and the Spirit, he cannot enter the kingdom of God. That which is born of flesh is flesh, and that which is born of the Spirit is spirit. Do not marvel that I said to you, you must be born again. The wind blows where it wishes and you hear the sound of it, but you cannot tell where it comes from or where it goes. So is everyone who is born of the Spirit"* (NKJV). Jesus uses water here as a symbol for the Word of God. Just as water cleanses something dirty, when we hear or read the Word, it shows us our lost condition and how we may be saved.

The second thing that must happen is God's Spirit dwelling inside us. This happens at the time of believing. The Holy Spirit indwells every person that is born again and gives the believer a capacity for spiritual things and the assurance of salvation. The same Holy Spirit teaches believers divine truths and shows people their sin at the time they believe and trust God's Spirit indwells them.

The third thing that must happen is personally believing on Christ, trusting Him as Savior and making Him the Lord of your life. By faith we know Him to be the substituted sacrifice for our sin.

How are we born again? Romans 3:23 says, *"For all have sinned and fall short of the glory of God"* (NKJV). All people have sinned against God. We are all born with a sin nature as a result of the fall of Adam and Eve. Therefore, people sin in their thoughts and actions. Only one man has not committed any sin in His entire life here on earth. That man is Jesus Christ. One might say, "I am a decent person" or "I follow the Ten Commandments," but the truth is, only Jesus was good, and we cannot follow the commandments completely. Only Jesus Christ was able to do that, for He committed no sin inwardly or outwardly.

James 2:10 says, *"For whoever shall keep the whole law, and yet stumble in one point, he is guilty of all"* (NKJV). So if a person has committed even just one sin, they fall short of God's standard. Even thinking that we are doing the best we can falls short. We find excuses for our failings. It's our nature, but Jesus said we have to be perfect to go to heaven (Matthew 5:48).

When God first created man (Adam), he was made perfect and innocent. Man was made in God's image. God not only created Adam physically alive but also spiritually alive. Man had perfect fellowship with God and His creation. When Adam listened to the devil and disobeyed God, he sinned and was separated from God forever. All mankind would now be born fallen in a fallen world. Because of the fall, Adam not only would die physically after a hard life, but he immediately died spiritually. Man was now mentally and spiritually depraved, full of guilt and shame. Man no longer sought after God and had no way to bring himself back to God. He could know about God, but not actually have a relationship with Him.

Man now lives for himself and does what he wants with no moral restraint. But God loves man so much that He provided a solution for man's predicament. Jesus was the only perfect man who ever lived. Why was Jesus a perfect man? Because He was both God and Man. Jesus was born of a virgin woman, and the Holy Spirit was His only true Father. Jesus existed before He was born a human on earth as the second person of the Godhead (Father, Son, and Holy Spirit). Because of that, He knew no sin, just as God cannot sin. This perfect man could then be the unblemished sacrifice required by God the Father to pay for all the sins of the world. Yet, as a man, Jesus was tempted and lived about thirty-three years as a normal human being.

If only perfect people go to heaven then we need a way to become perfect to satisfy God's requirement. Only through Jesus can that be done and people saved. I remember telling someone about Jesus, and the person saying to me, "I am a good person." Many people think that is enough to have eternal life. But God said no person is good.

Romans 3:10–12 says, *"There is none righteous, no, not one; There is none who understands; There is none who seeks after God. They have all turned aside; they have together become unprofitable; there is none who does good, no, not one"* (NKJV). We might seem good in our eyes, but not to a perfect, holy God. Man is destructive, disobedient, full of pride, boastful, immoral, and does not worship God as he should. These are some of the things we see, not to mention what goes on in the thought life of man, things such as anger and hate (Matthew 5:21–22).

People find many reasons to believe that they are all right with God and going to heaven. One reason they offer is "I go to church." What church? Who are they worshipping? Does going to church and doing good things in church mean a person is going to heaven? This is a good example of what is called works for salvation, which is not what the Bible teaches. Doing good deeds, baptism, giving money, etc., should be the result of our conversion and changed life, not a requirement to get salvation. The Bible does say in James 2:14–17 that good deeds, etc., come with faith and are evidence of a changed life. Saved, born again people do work as God calls them to because they are Christians. People cannot do works to be saved as many religions say and many people think. The Bible says so.

Ephesians 2:8–9 says, *"For by grace you have been saved through faith, and that not of yourselves; it is the gift of God, not of works, lest anyone should boast"* (NKJV). It is not what we have done but what God did for us. Some would say, "I am going to heaven when I die because I believe in God." Which god do they believe in? There are many gods in this world, and all but one are false imitations created by Satan and man. What do they believe about God? Most people say there is a God. Does that save them? Romans 1:20 says, *"For since the creation of the world His invisible attributes are clearly seen being understood by the things that are made, even His eternal power and Godhead, so that they are without excuse"* (NKJV). James 2:19 says, *"You believe there is one God. You do well. Even the demons believe—and tremble"* (NKJV)!

Scripture says that we can know there is a God by seeing His magnificent creation around us. Scripture also says that the demons believe and tremble. They will not go to heaven. What then does it mean by believe? What does it mean to have true, saving faith? What does it mean to trust in Jesus and be a Christian? It is by trusting in Jesus, who He is, and what He did for us that shows belief. Believing it with your mind and living it with your life is true faith. Only that kind of trust will qualify us for heaven. That is what Jesus meant by "believe." Living it with your life is sure evidence that you have repented, submitted to God, and asked Jesus to be the Lord of your life. A saved person shows true faith by a changed life and recognizes Jesus' call to obedience of His word.

John 15:5–8 says, *"Yes, I am the vine and you are the branches. Those who remain in me, and I in them, will produce much fruit. For apart from me you can do nothing. Anyone who parts from me is thrown away like a useless branch and withers. Such branches are gathered together in a pile to be burned. But if you stay joined to me and my words remain in you, you may ask any request you like, and it will be granted. My true disciples produce much fruit. This brings great glory to my Father"* (NLT).

Just as genuine salvation requires true faith, there is a faith that does not save. This faith may be sincere, but it does not save. In John 2:23–25, Jesus intentionally avoids a group of people who knew His name and knew that He was performing miracles. He knew that the faith they had was not saving faith. They did not wish to change.

John 12:42–43 says, *"Nevertheless even among the rulers many believed in Him. But because of the Pharisees they did not confess Him, lest they should be put out of the synagogue; for they loved the praise of men more than the praise of God"* (NKJV).

Many people use their ancestry, religion, philosophy, psychology, new age beliefs, and cults, thinking they are good as paths to God. Buddhism, Judaism, Hinduism, Islam, etc., are all false imitations designed or perverted by the devil to lead mankind astray, so he will be lost forever. The Bible says those paths are wrong, and we should not stubbornly cling to those beliefs. Jesus said that the road to heaven is narrow and few find it (Matthew 7:13). Jesus paid the full price for our sins, and God's love for us has provided a plan to escape hell and go to heaven. Jesus rose from the dead to prove He was the Son of God. Jesus said that the way to heaven was through Him. Too many people witnessed and saw Him after He rose for us not to believe He did!

When a person rejects God's free gift of salvation, they will face God's judgment. Judgment will result in eternal separation from God (damnation). Out of ignorance, some people may feel that's the way it is for them. They may even believe that they will be in hell with family and friends. Some think that they have been so bad that forgiveness is out of reach for them. Those who have that opinion are not aware of God's grace and love for them. God has provided some grace in their lives even now. The rain, the air we breathe, the food we eat, and Gods constant calling for our response to His gift of salvation are all examples of His grace. If you want Jesus to forgive you for the sins in your life, all you have to do is ask Him. His grace is truly amazing and He will forgive you. He loves you.

The Alternative

The alternative is what Scripture calls hell. We will be in one place or the other forever and know it. God created the universe, so it belongs to Him. He will share it with His creation out of His love for us and His Son. If people go to hell, it will be their choice, not Gods. They will have rejected God and His creation. Therefore, they will be put outside of it. This is a frightening truth. Praise God that He loves man and wants no one to go to hell. The world also has many popular views of what hell is and is not. Rather than saying what it is not, I will let Scripture and Jesus say what it is in the following verses:

"And the devil who deceived them, was thrown into the lake of burning sulfur, where the beast and false prophet had been thrown. They will be tormented day and night forever and ever" (Revelation 20:10, NIV)

"When the Son of man comes in His glory, and all the angels with Him, He will sit on His throne in heavenly glory. All the nations will be gathered before Him, and He will separate the people one from another as a shepherd separates the sheep from the goats. He will put the sheep on His right and the goats on His left" (Matthew 25:31, NIV).

"Then He will say to those on His left, Depart from Me, you who are cursed, into the fire prepared for the Devil and his angels" (Matthew 25:41, NIV).

"Then they will go away to eternal punishment, but the righteous to eternal life" (Matthew 25:46, NIV).

"And if your eye causes you to sin, pluck it out. It is better for you to enter the kingdom of God with one eye than to have two eyes and be thrown into hell, where their worm does not die, and the fire is not quenched" (Mark 9:47, NIV).

"For certain men, whose condemnation was written about long ago, have secretly slipped in among you. They are godless men, who change the grace of our God into license for immorality and deny Jesus Christ our only Sovereign and Lord. They are wild waves of the sea, foaming up their shame, wandering stars, for whom the blackest darkness has been reserved forever" (Jude 4, 13 NIV)

"Then death and Hades were thrown into the lake of fire. The lake of fire is the second death. If anyone's name was not found in the book of life, he was thrown into the lake of fire" (Revelation 20:14, NIV).

Jesus spoke a lot about hell when He was on earth among men. His love and sacrifice for man was to keep people from eternal punishment. Hell was created by God for the devil and his angels as a permanent holding place for them in the future. When in hell, they will no longer be able to cause the evil they did, which includes causing people to be deceived and lost eternally. Man, on the other hand, must respond to God to escape eternal damnation. He must decide to live eternally with God in His creation or have nothing to do with Him. We can respond to Him or forever exist in separation from God, which can only be in hell. From Scripture we can see that it is a place where life is separated from God, where it is dark, and where there is a type of fire that never goes out. It is a place where Jesus said their worm never dies and they are under torment eternally. That is a place no person should want to be forever. Praise God for the gift He offers us through His Son Jesus Christ. Just as we would want to protect our children, so has God devised a way to protect and save us, His children.

God does not change, and He does not sin. God separates Himself from sin and will judge those who do not take His gift of salvation. Mankind is born into this earth separated from God. We are selfish, boastful, immoral, full of pride, and disobedient, and we fail to worship God as we should.

Because of Adam's and Eve's fall, man's connection and unity with God, with other people, with himself, and with nature was separated. Only through God's divine plan and love for mankind will these connections and unities be repaired. Through Christ, these disconnects can be restored to how God created them to be. Romans 6:23 says, *"For the wages of sin is death, but the gift of God is eternal life in Christ Jesus our Lord"* (NKJV).

Because of man's sin nature, he is destined for eternal damnation. But we see in John 3:16–17, *"For God so loved the world that He gave His only begotten Son, that whoever believes in Him should not perish but have everlasting life. For God did not send His Son into the world to condemn the world, but that the world through Him might be saved"* (NKJV).

The Time Is Now

Jesus said, concerning the road to heaven, in John 14:6, "I Am the way, the truth, and the life. No one comes to the Father except through me" (NKJV). There are not many paths to heaven. There is only one. It is a narrow path, and few find it (Matthew 7:13–14). Many will not understand and try to take other ways to heaven. What about you? Your spirit and soul will live for eternity somewhere, whether you believe it or not. After all, you are made in God's image; that includes your eternal existence. It is your response God wants. God wants you to be saved.

The time to respond is now. Some think they are not ready, but God does not want you to wait. He asks you to receive Him now and promises to help you work out those things that keep you from responding. God will meet you where you are in life; there is no preparing yourself for being born again. We are not promised life here on earth tomorrow. God may not give you another chance to respond. Anything can happen this day and age, and we can only respond while we are alive. Why wait when the abundant life, a life of joy and hope He promises, can be yours? You can pray this prayer or similar words right now:

Lord, I am sorry and repent of my sins. Please forgive me for my sins. I want to go to heaven. I believe You died for my sins and rose from the grave. Please be my Lord and Savior and put my name in the Book of Life. Help me to change. Guide my life and fill me with the Holy Spirit. Thank You for drawing me to Jesus for salvation. In Jesus' name, amen.

If you prayed that prayer, then you should tell another Christian that you did. Remember, it is not the prayer that saves you. Repenting means you have turned away from your sin. It means that you will make a serious attempt at following God. He has given you the free gift of eternal life and placed the Holy Spirit inside you, and He will be with you every step of the way. Salvation is not a quick, emotional decision you make and then back to your old life. Christianity is not a religion. It is a lifestyle with God in all you do. If you are in a Bible-believing church, tell the pastor or elder about your decision. If you don't have a church home, find one as soon as you can. Read the section on finding a church. Your first act of obedience to God is getting baptized. Also get involved in a good Bible study group.

It's time to start some good habits. Pray and spend time with God, get into the Word, find a Bible that's easy to read. Starting in the gospel of John and then the book of 1 John is a good idea. I also think this guide will help you as you study and grow in the Word.

If you did not pray this prayer or one like it because you still do not understand or find it hard to believe, I give you a challenge. I ask you to pray a prayer something like this:

God, if You really do exist, and if You really do love me as I am, I ask you to reveal Yourself and Your truth to me. Let that truth help me to respond. Help me to know for sure that Jesus is the true path. Amen.

Chapter 2

The True Believer's Assurance of Salvation

When a person is saved, he or she can usually remember the moment they received Christ as Savior.

Sometimes it is a gradual experience that cannot be remembered clearly. Some of us received Christ while we were children, which can also be hard to remember.

If you are born again, on the rest of the page below, briefly write out your salvation experience. Include things such as when you were saved and how you were saved. What caused you to respond to God's calling? Who or what did God use to bring you the gospel and get you to respond to Him? Why do you believe that you are going to heaven?

_____

_____

_____

_____

_____

_____

_____

_____

_____

_____

How does a person know without any doubt that they are saved? It is not by any feeling or sign you may have or want. It is by trusting what God says in His Word. God's Word says that if a person trusts in Jesus, the Son of God, they are saved and have eternal security. Their sins are forgiven, and they have life eternal. God does not lie. True believers are saved from the penalty of their past, present, and future sins. You have been adopted into God's family, the church, and have the rights of son-ship (see the story of the prodigal son in Luke 15:11–32). You now have an approachable Father (Galatians 4:6). You have the promises of Christ for His church, such as the Holy Spirit living inside and with you. As a saint, you will rule and reign with Him in eternity. You will see your desires change, such as wanting to worship, please and serve the Lord. Ephesians 2:8 says, *"For it is by grace you have been saved through faith—and this not from yourselves, it is a gift from God"* (NIV). John 5:24 says, *"I assure you, those who listen to my message and believe in God who sent me have eternal life. They will never be condemned for their sins, but they have already passed from death to life"* (NLT). Jude 24 says, *"To Him who is able to keep you from falling and to present you before His glorious presence without fault and with great joy"* (NIV).

Christians will someday be like Christ, and the presence of sin will no longer be with us. 1 John 3:2 says, *"Dear friends now we are children of God, and what we will be has not yet been made known. But we know that when He appears we shall be like Him, for we shall see Him as He is. Everyone who has this hope in Him purifies himself just as He is pure"* (NIV).

1. Read Romans 6:1–16. When you became a Christian, two things happened to you. What does verse six say they are?

_____

_____

_____

_____

According to verse eleven, how must you consider yourself?

_____

_____

_____

_____

Verse thirteen says you, as a Christian, have a responsibility. What is it?

_____

_____

_____

_____

What determines whether you are a slave to sin or to righteousness in verse sixteen?

_____

_____

_____

_____

2 Peter 1:3–4 says, *"As we know Jesus better, His divine power gives us everything we need for living a godly life. He has called us to receive His own glory and goodness! And by that same mighty power, He has given us all of His rich and wonderful promises. He has promised that you will escape the decadence all around you caused by evil desires and that you will share in His divine nature"* (NLT).

Hebrews 9:28 says, *"So also Christ died only once as a sacrifice to take away the sins of many people. He will come again but not to deal with our sins again. This time He will bring the completion of salvation to all those who are eagerly waiting for Him"* (NLT).

We as Christians believe that by God's grace we have been saved by Him. We believe it not to be because of anything we have done but that it is a gift from God. That is what God's Word tells us. Because you have been redeemed through Jesus Christ, God has satisfied His justice and the penalty for sin. His Son paid the penalty for your sin through the cross and all it entailed. Therefore, you have been justified. By His grace and mercy you have been given this free gift. Instead of God's wrath falling on you, His anger and wrath for your sin fell upon Jesus at the cross. Because you are redeemed and justified, you must believe it by faith. That means you should trust that it is true. Jesus is now your object of faith. You believe what He did for you, and you live your life based on that. You trust Him in every way. Jesus did it, and you receive it.

Romans 3:22–26 says, *"This righteousness from God comes through faith in Jesus Christ to all who believe. There is no difference, for all have sinned and fall short of the glory of God, and are justified freely by His grace through the redemption that came by Christ Jesus. God presented Him as a sacrifice of atonement, through faith in His blood. He did this to demonstrate His justice, because in His forbearance He had left the sins committed beforehand unpunished. He did it to demonstrate His justice at the present time, so as to be just and the one who justifies those who have faith in Jesus"* (NIV).

See what the following verses say about your salvation and the assurance that you are saved.

2. What has God done for us by our faith in Romans 5:1–2?

_____

_____

_____

_____

3. What does the Word say about our salvation in 1 John 5:11–12?

_____

_____

_____

_____

4. According to 1 Corinthians 6:11, by what are we made right with God?

_____

_____

_____

_____

5. How can you know you are a child of God, according to Galatians 4:6 and Romans 8:16?

_____

_____

6. In Romans 8:1, what do we not have after receiving Christ?

_____

_____

_____

_____

7. What is it that we may know, and why, according to 1 John 5:13?

_____

_____

_____

_____

8. What have you become, according to 2 Corinthians 5:17?

_____

_____

_____

_____

What do you see in your life that shows you are a new creation and that old things have or are passing away?

_____

_____

_____

_____

When a person is unsaved or not born again, they are spiritually dead. They have no means of understanding spiritual things or making spiritual decisions because they are fallen. Romans 3:10–11 says, *"As it is written, there is none righteous, not even one. There is none who understands. There is none who seeks for God"* (NKJV).

9. Read Romans 3:12–18 and write down what the apostle Paul says.

_____

_____

_____

Man is depraved in his unsaved condition and needs outside help in order to be saved. We cannot decide to be saved in our fallen condition, just as we cannot decide to be unsaved if we are born again. That is why salvation is the work of God and His grace alone! This should give us our greatest assurance and joy. Our salvation is not based on how we feebly hold on to God. It is based on God's firm grasp on us and that He will *never* let go. If you are truly born again, you will never lose your salvation! God loves you so much He initiated your salvation and will sustain it forever and ever. You will grow in your love for God and want to obey Him as you mature in Him.

Ephesians 2 8-10 says, *"For by grace you have been saved through faith and that not of yourselves, it is the gift of God, not as a result of works, so that no one may boast. For we are His workmanship, created in Christ Jesus for good works which God prepared beforehand so that we would walk in them"* (NKJV).

In John 6:44–45, Jesus says, *"No man can come to Me unless the Father who sent Me draws him; and I will raise him up on the last day. It is written in the prophets, and they shall all be taught of God. Everyone who has heard and learned from the Father comes to Me"* (NKJV).

In these verses, we see that by God's grace and power, His Word (the gospel) produced saving faith in those of us that are saved and trusted what He said was true. The faith came about when we heard and learned about God and salvation (the gospel). This is the Father drawing and teaching us, as Jesus said. By the Holy Spirit, all who hear Him and believe because the Word of God reaches their spiritual hearts are those who come to Jesus and are born again. Those that do not trust the gospel to be true are unbelievers. They will die in their sin; they will not be saved. They have no desire to be saved and have rejected God. They are actually held captive by the devil and sin.

God paid the price for the whole world (John 3:16), but not all people will really hear God calling when they are given the Word. We must always pray that God will reach them. He is the God of second chances. If God did not draw man to Himself, no one would come. Salvation is indeed the work of God from before creation, to Jesus' atoning death on the cross, and into eternity. Man's hope lies outside himself. It relies on God's love, mercy, and grace.

10. Read John 6:37 and write down what Jesus said in the space below.

---

11. According to John 6:38–40, what is the will of the Father for sending Jesus to mankind?

That is so amazing! The Scripture says God the Father chose us first by drawing us because we were unable to choose Him. We were drawn by the gospel, which the Father by His Spirit gave to us, using someone, some circumstance, or the Scripture. Then God the Father gives us to His Son Jesus who He sent to earth to redeem mankind. We then come to Jesus. Jesus receives all the people that the Father gives Him. Jesus also will never lose anyone the Father has given Him. He will keep us forever. But that's not the end of it—Jesus will resurrect us in the last day and give us eternal life. God also will make us like Jesus. Wow, just as Jesus was foreordained from the foundation of the world to go to the cross and be the sacrifice for man, so are true believers predestined to be chosen by God for salvation. This means that God chose you to have eternal life with Him in His kingdom before He created the universe.

1 Peter 1:2 says, *"Peter an apostle of Jesus Christ, to those who reside as aliens, scattered throughout Pontus, Galatia, Cappadocia, Asia, and Bithynia, who **are chosen** according to the **foreknowledge of God the Father**, by the sanctifying work of the Spirit, **to obey Jesus Christ and be sprinkled with His blood**: May grace and peace be yours in the fullest measure"* (NKJV).

Because a true believer is saved, he or she is justified by faith alone based on God's grace. There is nothing that can be held against you. There is no condemnation, as it says in Romans 8:1.

12. Read Romans 8:29–39 and put in your own words what these verses say.

_____

_____

_____

_____

List the ten things Paul says can never separate us from the love of God in Romans 8:38–39.

_____

_____

_____

_____

Does anything in life not fit in one of these ten categories? What can separate you from God?

_____

_____

_____

_____

Another way of knowing that we are born again is by our walk with Him. Our walk with Him encompasses many facets. It includes our obedience, our bearing of fruit, our love for others, especially believers, our relationship with God, and most importantly, our love for God.

1John 2:3–4 says, *"We know that we have come to know Him if we obey His commands. The man who says, 'I know Him,' but does not do what He commands is a liar, and the truth is not in Him"* (NIV).

John 15:9–17 says, *"As the Father has loved Me so have I loved you. Now remain in My love. If you obey My commands you will remain in My love. Just as I have obeyed My Father's commands and remain in His love. I have told you this so that My joy may be in you and that your joy may be complete. My command is this: Love each other as I have loved you. Greater love has no one than this that He lay down His life for His friends. You are my friends if you do what I command. I no longer call you servants because a servant does not know his master's business. Instead, I have called you friends, for everything that I learned from My Father I have made known to you. You did not choose me, but I chose you and appointed you to go and bear fruit—fruit that will last. Then the Father will give you whatever you ask in My name. This is My command: Love each other"* (NIV).

13. According to John 15: 1–8, what do we have to do to bear fruit?

_____

_____

_____

_____

What happens when we do not bear fruit?

_____

_____

_____

_____

What does it mean that no branch (person) can bear fruit by itself?

_____

_____

_____

_____

How can these verses in John 15 show us that we are Christians?

_____

_____

_____

_____

14. What does James say about the Word in James 1:22?

_____

_____

_____

So, we see that there are evidences in our lives that show that we are truly born again. Evidences such as being obedient to His Word, bearing fruit, and our personal walk with Him. It does not mean that if we are saved we can live any way we want. Is the pattern of your sin diminished when compared to your old life? Are you starting to see victory over your sin? Do you truly believe Christ is the true God? Are you confessing your sin? Do you believe you have eternal life? Does the Holy Spirit inside you affirm you are a child of God? Do you desire to read the Word, pray, and spend time with God and other believers? True believers follow His Word because they love God more than anything in life. If you are not saved but believe and trust His Word to be true then ask Jesus to be your Lord and Savior.

John 10:27–30 says, _"My sheep hear My voice, and I know them and they follow Me; and I give eternal life to them and they will never perish; and no one will snatch them out of My hand. My Father who has given them to Me is greater than all; and no one is able to snatch them out of the Father's hand. I and the Father are one"_ (NKJV). Pray:

Lord, I thank you for the magnificent truths in your Word about my eternal life. I am chosen by you and will always be in your family. Sometimes I may have doubts about my salvation. But you cannot lie, and your Word says I was saved when I responded to you, asked you to be my Savior and Lord, and repented of my sin. Please continue to give me confidence and strength. Help me to have a great desire to trust you and to be obedient. Help me to love you and learn more of your ways as each day passes. Lord, I give you now all my worries, my sin, hidden sin, health issues, money issues, failures, and other problems. I lift it all up and give it to you. Thank you for your peace and joy. In the name of Jesus, amen.

In the beginning of this chapter, you wrote out your salvation experience. Studying the book of 1 John is excellent for giving you the confidence that you have eternal life with God. **Are there any insights after reviewing this chapter that you would add? Write them below.**

Chapter 3

The Bible

God has given to man a written revelation about Himself and His creation. This love letter tells us about God's absolute truths concerning Jesus Christ, His son, and His love for mankind. The Bible talks about God's plan for the redemption of man as well as how we should live. It tells us about the result of sin, death, and eternal existence. In the Bible, we read how we can communicate with God and how He communicates with us. The Bible shows us how to deal with fear and guilt. In the Bible, we learn the commandment that all life hangs on is to love God with all our hearts and to love others as ourselves (Mark 12:30).

Although we see the Bible as one book, it is actually comprised of sixty-six separate books starting with the book of Genesis and ending with the book of Revelation. These books are divided into two main parts. The first thirty-nine books are called the Old Testament, and the remaining twenty-seven books are called the New Testament. One thing that is always true for the Old and New Testaments is that Jesus is the central figure. The Bible should be read with that in mind.

The Bible was written in different eras under the inspiration and supernatural revelation of God by many authors. This is a miracle in itself. These people wrote Scripture in different eras, in three different languages, all to be compiled to make one smooth, flowing book that speaks of life and God. These writers wrote about the events they witnessed and used inspired writings that were already in existence, and God gave them those words to record. The words were carefully translated and copied from early scrolls and manuscripts. Many manuscripts and archaeological tablets still exist today to show these geographical, historical, cultural, and spiritual truths. These ancient manuscripts show us that the wording of our modern Bible is very accurate. These manuscripts, however, did not have the chapter and verse numbers we see today. These were added later as help for the readers. There have been over 24,000 manuscripts for the Bible to show its truth. In spite of that, attacks to the Bible's accuracy still occur. No wonder that today people would readily accept the life of Julius Caesar to be accurate, for which there are only about ten manuscripts.

The manuscripts and scrolls were later compiled into one book (canonicity) under stringent criteria. The criterion they used was whether the books had apostolic authority. Was the criteria used by the early churches? Did they teach sound doctrine? Books that did not meet criteria were not added, such as the many apocryphal books in existence.

Prophecy is another way we see that the Bible is true. Over three hundred prophecies about Christ's life, His death, and what He did while God in the flesh came true in Scripture and life. Prophecy in the Bible about the nation Israel and other people and events all came true. Just food for thought—if these prophecies came true, what about those that have yet to happen? Many have yet to happen, such as prophecy about God's people, the tribulation, heaven, hell, eternity, etc. About one third of Scripture is prophecy. Every word was written under the inspiration of God.

After about AD 90, most Scripture, which we call the Bible, was completed. It is not fair for us to reason that the Bible was written in part by man and part by God. Then we would be saying that the Bible is only partially inspired. The whole Bible is the Word of God.

The Bible is different from other religious, philosophical, or theological books. The Bible is also not just a book of ideas. The Bible is rooted in the actual lives of people and history, inspired by God. To a world without Christ, the Bible is just a book because, without the Holy Spirit, a person cannot fully comprehend it. One must be saved to have the Holy Spirit help reveal the truths of the Bible. Even a child who is filled with the Spirit will understand it.

"All Scripture is given by the inspiration of God, and is profitable for doctrine, for reproof, for correction, for instruction in righteousness, that the man of God may be complete, thoroughly equipped for every good work" (2 Timothy 3:16–17, NKJV).

The Old Testament

The first five books of the Old Testament are called the Pentateuch. These books written by Moses start with the beginning of time and creation, the stories of the patriarchs, and God's people chosen to give the good news of God's redemptive plan to a world perishing because of sin. From the very first pages in Genesis, it is said that Jesus, who is the seed of the woman, will suffer but will crush Satan's head at the cross.

1. Write the first five books of the Old Testament, which are referred to as the Pentateuch or the books of the law.

G_____ This book is about creation, sin, redemption, and Israel.

E_____ This book is about God's people being delivered from Egypt.

L_____ This book is about sacrifice, atonement, and worship.

N_____ This is about Israel's wanderings for forty years.

D_____ This book is about the preparation for the Promised Land.

The next twelve books from Joshua to Esther are about the history of Israel and God's dealing with His chosen nation. The following five books of the Old Testament are the books of poetry: Job, Psalms, Proverbs, Ecclesiastes, and the Song of Solomon. They include instruction, songs of praise, wisdom for living, etc. The books of the Major Prophets follow the poetry books. These are the books of Isaiah, Jeremiah, Lamentations, Ezekiel, and Daniel. They are followed by the books of the Minor Prophets, which are called that because they are shorter in length. There are twelve from the book of Hosea to the book of Malachi, which is the last book of the Old Testament. Jesus Himself quoted the writings of the Old Testament. For example, Jesus mentioned Jonah. He had knowledge in speaking about Abraham, Isaac, and Jacob. Jesus showed that He believed Scripture to be the Word of God. God revealed Himself by inspiring men to write Scripture.

2. What did Jesus say in Matthew 5:17–18 and John 5:39 concerning Himself and the Old Testament prophesies?

_____

_____

_____

_____

3. Where did Peter say the Old Testament writings came from in 2 Peter 1:21 and Acts 1:16?

_____

_____

_____

_____

The New Testament

The New Testament starts with the four gospels, which include the heart of our Christian walk. They focus on Jesus and who He is, what He did for mankind, and the eternal outcome of man.

Write the four gospels in order.

M_____ This book reveals the life of Jesus and communicates to the Jews that He is the true Messiah of the Scriptures.

M_____ This book shows the life of Christ and is written to reveal Jesus as the obedient servant.

L_____ This gospel is written to the Greek world revealing that Jesus was the perfect man—the way man was created to be. It shows the life of Jesus and His humanity.

J_____ This gospel shows Jesus as the only begotten Son of God. The book shows His life and deity.

4. What does Jesus say concerning the following Scriptures? What does He say about those who did not believe Him?

Luke 24:25–27

_____

_____

_____

_____

Luke 24:44–48

_____

_____

_____

_____

5. In Acts 3:18, what did Peter say about Jesus and Scripture?

_____

_____

_____

_____

Following the gospels, we come to the beginning of the Church as well as the history of the early Church in the book of Acts. After the book of Acts, the next twenty-one books are called the epistles. These books are letters written to churches and individuals concerning the Christian walk, faith, and responsibility.

Revelation, the last book of the New Testament, is mostly a prophetic book. It contains messages from Jesus to the churches. The book speaks about the coming of Christ, His reign as king, His Glory, the Glory of the Father, and the eternal state of believers as well as unbelievers.

Scripture is often called God's Word because, as believers, we know God is speaking to us. Through His Word He comforts, He corrects, and helps us make decisions. We see answers to prayer in His Word. We also read about many examples of life in the Bible, such as Jesus using Scripture and what the Word says about our temptations.

6. In Matthew 4:4–10, what did Christ reference as authority to answer Satan's attacks?

_____

_____

_____

_____

7. What does Scripture say in 1 Corinthians 10:13 about our temptations?

_____

_____

_____

_____

To sum it up, we should read the Bible and study it slowly and carefully. We should memorize verses for ourselves and to help others. We should not just know what it says, but apply what we learn. We should ask God to help us understand, by His Holy Spirit, what it says. The Bible tells us about the heart of God and His love for us. It will give you an eternal perspective when you read and hear it. You will learn to live with a biblical worldview when you study it. In it, we see how to be saved and be assured of who we are in Him. God will speak to you through the Bible. As a Christian, God will guide and light your path as you study His Word.

In studying Scripture, pray first and ask God to give you understanding and reveal the truths He wants you to learn. Start by reading the content of the passages you are studying. Then read it again, underlining key passages and words. You may want to read several Bible translations to get a better understanding. A Bible dictionary, concordance, and commentary can also help. Pay close attention to who, what, where, why, how, and when. Then write down what the passage is teaching. After that, ask yourself what the passage means to you. What action do you need to take? Are there sins to confess? Is there a promise for you in the passage? Is God telling you to avoid something, or is there an answer to a prayer there? What examples are there to follow? What other personal applications does God have for you in the passage? Here is a prayer you can use before Bible study: **Father in heaven, please give me a great desire to read and study Your Word. Teach me Your ways and show me Your will for my life. Help me to remember what I study in Your Word and to apply it to my life. In the name of Jesus, amen.**

Chapter 4

God

God has always existed. The Scripture says in Psalm 14:1, *"The fool has said in his heart that there is no God"* (NKJV). The Bible itself does not try to prove God's existence; it just makes it a point of fact. Although we cannot fully fathom the nature of God, the Bible does tell us some things we can understand. The word "trinity," for example, is not in the Bible, yet there is truth in Scripture that helps us understand the concept.

The following Scriptures tells us there is one God with three persons in the Godhead—Father, Son, and Holy Spirit. In Romans 1:7, the Father is called God: *"To all who are in Rome, beloved of God, called to be saints. Grace to you and peace from God our Father and the Lord Jesus Christ"* (NKJV). The Son is called God, by the Father, in Hebrews 1:8: *"But of the Son He says: Your throne O God is forever and ever; a scepter of righteousness is the scepter of your kingdom"* (NKJV). The Holy Spirit is called God in Acts 5:3–4: *"But Peter said, 'Ananias why has Satan filled your heart to lie to the Holy Spirit and keep back part of the price of the land for yourself? While it remained was it not your own? And after it was sold was it not in your own control? Why have you conceived this thing in your heart? You have not lied to men but to God'"* (NKJV).

When you look up Matthew 3:16–17, Matthew 28:19 and 2 Corinthians 13:14, you will see that the Father, Son, and Holy Spirit are all present. God said, "I AM WHO I AM" in Exodus 3:14. It is not possible for us to define God. We can only see some of the qualities He has, and they are all perfect. God is omnipresent, which means He is everywhere at the same time.

Jeremiah 23:24 says, *"'Can anyone hide himself in secret places, so I shall not see him? says the Lord; Do I not fill heaven and earth?' says the Lord"* (NKJV).

God is also omniscient, meaning He knows all things. He knows all our thoughts and actions— all His creation and everything down to every molecule in existence. He knows everything about everything. God is omnipotent, which means He is all-powerful. All of creation is held together by His power. Matthew 19:26 says, *"But Jesus looked at them and said to them, 'With men this is impossible, but with God all things are possible'"* (NKJV).

God is Holy. He hates sin and is sinless. God's holiness separates Him from sin as at the fall of Adam and Eve. He separated Himself from His fallen creation, but He had a plan to bring back the harmony He had with man and His creation through Jesus Christ because His purposes cannot be thwarted, Isaiah 59:1–2 says, *"Behold the Lord's hand is not shortened that it cannot save; nor His ear heavy that it cannot hear. But your iniquities have separated you from your God; and your sins have hidden His face from you"* (NKJV).

God is Love. God loves the sinner, although He hates sin. Because of sin, man is destined for hell. John 3:16 says, *"For God so loved the world that He gave His only begotten Son that whoever believes in Him should not perish but have everlasting life"* (NKJV).

God does not change. The God of the Old Testament is the same God of the New Testament. He is the same from eternity past to eternity future. In Malachi 3:6, God says, *"I the Lord do not change"* (NIV).

God is just. Everything God does is for good. Everything He does is right and fair. God does not lie, so He fulfills all He says. Psalm 119:137 says, *"Righteous are you, O Lord, and upright are your judgments"* (NKJV).

Jesus Christ

To the world, Jesus is believed to have many descriptions. Some people think He was crazy and a lunatic. Others say He is the archangel Michael or a prophet, that He was a good person or some kind of spiritual leader. In Matthew 16:15, Jesus asked His disciples who they thought He was. Peter answered and said He was the Son of God, and indeed He is, in His human form.

Jesus is the second person of the Trinity. The first two chapters of Genesis talk about God creating all things. In the first few verses in the gospel of John, we see who Jesus is, and we also see how He was involved in creation and man's redemption: *"In the beginning was the Word, and the Word was with God, and the Word was God. He was in the beginning with God. All things were made through Him, and without Him nothing was made that was made. In Him was life, and the life was the light of men. And the light shines in the darkness and the darkness did not understand it. And the Word became flesh and dwelt among us, and we beheld His glory, the glory as of the only begotten of the Father, full of grace and truth"* (John 1: 1–5, 14, NKJV).

This tells us that Jesus is God. He came into this world by being conceived by the Holy Spirit through a virgin birth, and as a man, He lived a sinless life. Jesus did not cease to be God while He was a man. Although Jesus is God, He chose to put aside His deity to become a man for the sake of revealing the Father and for mans' redemption. He showed He is God by allowing man to put Him to death and supernaturally raising Himself back to life.

Hebrews 2:17 says, *"For this reason He had to be made like His brothers in every way, in order that He might become a merciful and faithful high priest in service to God, and that He might make atonement for the sins of the people"* (NIV).

As a man, Jesus was totally submissive to the Father. Because He was a man, He had feelings, emotions, sorrow, hunger, and temptations, and He knew what it was to be a man.

1. Rewrite what it says about Jesus in Philippians 2:7–8.

_____

_____

_____

_____

When Jesus was in the flesh as a man, John 20:28 says He was recognized by men and worshiped. In Mark 1: 24, He was also recognized by demons as the Son of God.

2. What does Jesus declare himself to be in John 10:30?

_____

_____

_____

_____

3. What three works of God were performed by Jesus in John 1:3, Colossians 1:16, and John 2:19?

_____

_____

_____

_____

4. What do Matthew 28:20, Revelation 1:18, John 21:17 and John 17:5 say about the attributes of Jesus?

_____

_____

_____

_____

5. What was predicted about Jesus in Isaiah 7:14 and what was said about Jesus in Hebrews 10:7?

_____

_____

_____

_____

There are over three hundred Old Testament prophecies written about Jesus. They were written hundreds of years before they happened. Following are some of those prophecies and their fulfillments in the New Testament:

Isaiah 7:14, Luke 1: 34-35—born of a virgin
Micah 5:2, Luke 2:4–7— born in Bethlehem
Isaiah 11:2, Matthew 3:16–17—anointed by the Holy Spirit
Psalm 34:20, John 19: 32–36—none of His bones broken
Psalm 118:22, 1 Peter 2:7—rejected by His own
Psalm 69:9, Matthew 21:12—cleanses the temple
Zechariah 12:10, John 19:34—His side is pierced
Psalm 16:8-11, Matthew 28:6—rose from the dead
Psalm 68:18, Acts 1:9—ascended to heaven

6. The Bible says that Christ came to this world in human form in order to do what?

John 14:9

_____

_____

_____

_____

1 John 3:8

_____

_____

_____

_____

Hebrews 9:26

_____

_____

_____

_____

1 Corinthians 15:3

_____

_____

_____

_____

As a man, Jesus spoke out against the misconceptions that the people had developed concerning the ceremonial laws, civil laws, and moral laws. He taught about the major issues of life on earth and in heaven that God had given. He taught about unknown things (John 11:24–26) and that the Father was sovereign. He revealed the Father by what He taught and how He lived. He showed man the nature of God. He taught Gods' purpose for man and that man is to have a servant's loving heart. He taught that man should glorify God. Jesus declared promises, such as the following:

Though you have not seen Him, you love Him; and even though you do not see Him now, you believe in Him and are filled with an inexpressible and glorious joy, for you are receiving the goal of your faith, the salvation of your soul (1 Peter 1:8–9, NIV)

But the counselor, the Holy Spirit, whom the Father will send in My name, will teach you all things and will remind you of everything I have said to you (John 14:26, NIV).

I have given you authority to trample on snakes and scorpions and to overcome all the power of the enemy; nothing will harm you. However, do not rejoice that the spirits submit to you, but rejoice that your names are written in heaven (Luke 10:19-20, NIV).

I tell you the truth, if anyone keeps my word, he will never see death (John 8:51, NIV).

After Christ's death for mankind, He was resurrected in order to complete the work of the cross and fulfill prophecy (Romans 4:25). He now carries out His Priestly position representing His people seated at the right side of the Father. Hebrews 4:14–16 says, *"Seeing then that we have a great High Priest who has passed through the heavens, Jesus the Son of God, let us hold fast our confession. For we do not have a High Priest who cannot sympathize with our weaknesses, but was in all points tempted as we are, yet without sin. Let us therefore come boldly to the throne of grace that we may obtain mercy and grace to help in time of need"* (NKJV).

Jesus' resurrected body was real. It was not a spirit. John 20:27 says you could see the markings in His body from His crucifixion. Even though His body was real, it was also changed and did not appear to have any limitations. He appeared to more than five hundred reliable witnesses after His resurrection (1 Corinthians 15:6). We must realize that without the resurrection, there is no Christian faith. We would also have no hope of resurrection and eternal life. Life would be in vain.

When His work was finished on earth, Christ was seen by witnesses ascending to the Father in heaven (Acts 1:9). Jesus reigns today in the hearts of His believers. In the future millennium, He will reign as King of kings and Lord of lords.

7. Psalm 72 describes Christ as the reigning king. List some aspects of the Lord's reign.

The Holy Spirit

The third person of the Godhead is the Holy Spirit. Jesus promised believers that He would send the Holy Spirit (the Comforter) after He ascended to the Father. The Holy Spirit indwells all Christians when they are saved, but not all believers are fully controlled by Him. When we as true believers have surrendered our wills totally, have put out of our lives all known sin, have strived to be obedient, and have sought to be filled by the power of the Holy Spirit, the Spirit is free to do His will in us. The Spirit that indwells us now fully fills us. The Holy Spirit may then do what God intended in a Christian's life.

When Jesus walked this earth, He was with man physically. He showed the Father through Himself. Now that He has risen, He shows Himself through the Holy Spirit and comes to us through the Spirit. John 14:18 says, *"I will not leave you as orphans; I will come to you"* (NASB). In John 14:9, Jesus says, *"Have I been so long with you, and yet you have not come to know Me, Philip? He who has seen Me has seen the Father; how can you say, 'Show us the Father?'"* (NASB). The Holy Spirit is not a force or a power. He is God.

8. How do the following Scriptures describe the attributes of the Holy Spirit?

Isaiah 40:13–14

_____

_____

_____

_____

Psalm 139:7

_____

_____

_____

_____

Hebrews 9:14

_____

_____

_____

_____

The fact that the Holy Spirit has feelings and emotions is shown in the following verse: *Do not grieve the Holy Spirit of God, by whom you were sealed for the day of redemption* (Ephesians 4:30, NASB).

9. What does 1 Corinthians 12:7–11 say the Holy Spirit does for believers?

_____

_____

_____

_____

10. What did the Holy Spirit say to the church in Acts 13:2 that shows He makes decisions as God?

_____

_____

_____

_____

Of the many things the Holy Spirit does, there are four main ministries concerning people. He abides inside believers. He brings glory and points only to Jesus Christ. He intercedes for us, according to God's will. He comforts believers, convicts, and moves in hearts of people to guide them, and He reveals God to unbelievers.

First, He abides in those who receive Jesus as their Savior and Lord at the time of their salvation. At this time, Scripture says the Holy Spirit is with us, in us, and can overflow in us; these are described as the fullness of the Spirit or Baptism of the Spirit.

11. What do the following Scriptures say about what the Holy Spirit does in us when we are saved?

1 Corinthians 3:16

_____

_____

_____

_____

John 14:16–17

_____

_____

_____

_____

John 7:38–39

_____

_____

_____

_____

John 3:5

_____

_____

_____

_____

1 Corinthians 12:13

_____

_____

_____

_____

Ephesians 4:30

_____

_____

_____

_____

Romans 8:16

_____

_____

_____

_____

12. What does Paul say about our bodies in 1 Corinthians 6:19?

_____

_____

_____

_____

When we asked Jesus to be our Savior and Lord, we invited the Holy Spirit to live within us. You may ask yourself how the Holy Spirit can live inside me when I seem to be so unholy. This is why Jesus came to do what He did. Jesus died for us on the cross and ascended to the Father. By what He did, Jesus was glorified. By faith, we believe in Him, what He did, and our salvation. So, Jesus sends to us the Holy Spirit. We are holy because of Jesus. By this, then, the Holy Spirit is free to indwell us. John 7:38–39 says, *"He who believes in Me, as the scripture said, From his innermost being will flow rivers of living water. But this He spoke of the Spirit, whom those who believed in Him were to receive; for the Spirit was not yet given, because Jesus was not yet glorified"* (NASB). In Titus 3:5–6, we read, *"He saved us not on the bases of deeds which we have done in righteousness, but according to His mercy, by the washing of regeneration and renewing by the Holy Spirit, whom He poured out upon us richly through Jesus Christ our Savior"* (NASB).

13. Because you are saved, you have the Holy Spirit in you. Are you letting the Holy Spirit have His way? What is His purpose in your life?

_____

_____

_____

_____

Second, the Holy Spirit points to and glorifies Jesus Christ; this is one of the main reasons He was sent. John 16:14 says, *"He will glorify Me, for He will take of Mine and will disclose it to you"* (NASB). Just as the Holy Spirit glorifies Jesus, He also wants us to be totally submitted to Jesus. We are to be preoccupied with Him 24/7. We are to glorify and point to Jesus as well.

14. What does the Holy Spirit do for us in Romans 8:27?

_____

_____

_____

In John 16:15?

_____

_____

_____

_____

Third, the Spirit convicts, comforts, and moves in hearts to convince people. The Spirit teaches and convinces us about the truth concerning Jesus. That He is Lord of all. That He is the only path to salvation. He convicts us of sin. He shows us that with salvation comes forgiveness. Through Him, we understand Scripture and remember what He has taught us.

The Spirit comforts us. He shows us God's mercy and grace. He cleanses us from sin and teaches us to trust Jesus. Our joy comes from Him as He is with us through our lives and with us forever. John 14:26 says, *"But the Helper the Holy Spirit, Whom the Father will send in My name, He will teach you all things and bring to your remembrance all that I said to you"* (NASB). John16:12–15 says, *"I have many more things to say to you, but you cannot bear them now. But when He, the Spirit of truth, comes, He will guide you into all the truth, for He will not speak on His own initiative, but whatever He hears, He will speak, and He will disclose to you what is to come. He will glorify Me, for He will take of Mine and will disclose it to you. All things that the Father has are Mine; therefore I said that He takes of Mine and will disclose it to you"* (NASB).

15. What does 1 Corinthians 2:10–13 say about what the Holy Spirit does, what He searches, and what He knows?

_____

_____

_____

_____

_____

Being Fully Controlled by the Holy Spirit

We already covered the fact that we are filled with the Holy Spirit when saved, but we must totally submit (surrender) our lives to God to be controlled by Him and to see Him work in our lives. When we do not do this, we have less joy in our Christian life. We tend to lose interest in telling others about Jesus and even lose the desire. But when we do surrender totally to God, these things come back as well as seeing victory over sin and God moving in our prayer lives. Surrender means obedience and giving God all we are and have. Selfishness, unbelief, the love for things, money, unholy actions, anger, self-praise, and dishonesty are only some of the attitudes people may have that will keep the Holy Spirit from totally controlling and filling them. The Holy Spirit works through clean vessels.

Galatians 5:16–17 says, *"But I say walk by the Spirit, and you will not carry out the desires of the flesh. For the flesh sets its desire against the Spirit, and the Spirit against the flesh; for these are in opposition to one another, so you may not do the things that you please"* (NASB).

16. Read the following verses and write the things that keep the Holy Spirit from completely controlling and working through us.

Luke 9:26

_____

_____

_____

_____

Prov. 16:18

_____

_____

_____

Psalm 66:18

_____

_____

_____

_____

1 John 2:15–17

_____

_____

_____

_____

17. What are the things that you need to pray about that come between you and God to prevent you from being totally controlled and filled by the Holy Spirit?

_____

_____

_____

_____

Who is ruling your life?

_____

_____

_____

18. Being filled and controlled by the Spirit is also a matter of faith (trust) that He has done so. How can we know this has actually happened?

_____

_____

_____

_____

19. What does it mean to you that every true believer is filled with the Spirit but not controlled by the Spirit?

_____

_____

_____

_____

The Names of God

The Bible describes God with many names. These names all have a meaning for what God does or who He is. When we study these names we learn about God's character, His uniqueness, and His love for mankind. Below are many of these names with Scripture references and meanings:

YHWH "I AM" Exodus 3:14–15, Malachi 3:6—God is faithful and never changes. He keeps His promises. He is the only God who is and has made Himself known to man. He is self-existent as God, with no beginning or end. He is the center of all things, not man. He is the uncaused cause of all things that exist.

ADONAI "Lord, Master" Psalm 2:4, Isaiah 40:3–5—God is Lord. God is Master, and God is sovereign.

EL "The strong one" Deuteronomy 7:9, Mark 15:34—We can depend on God. He overcomes all obstacles.

EL-BERITH Judges 9:46—He is God of the covenant.

EL-ELYON "God most high" Genesis 14:18–23, Psalm 78:35—He does not change and is the God in whom we can trust.

EL-OLAM "The eternal God; Everlasting God" Genesis 21:33, Isaiah 40:28—He is the Alpha and Omega. He gives strength to the weak.

EL-SHADDAI "All powerful God," "The God almighty" Genesis 35:11, Psalm 90:2, Genesis 17:1–8, Isaiah 49:5-6, Psalm 138:7-8—God is the source of our blessings. God is almighty. He is all-sufficient, transcendent, and sovereign God. He is our strength.
EL-ELOHE YISRAEL "The God of Israel" Genesis 33:20—The God of Israel is separate from all other false gods.

ELOHIM "All powerful Creator" Psalm 68, Mark 13:19, Deuteronomy 6:4, Isaiah 45:18, 46:8–9—This is the second most used name of God in Scripture. God is everywhere, knows all, is all-powerful, and is creator of all. He is strong and mighty. He is full of majesty and splendor. This name is revealed as a plurality. He has the power to execute His will and nothing can stop it. This makes Him worthy to be feared.

EL ROI "God who sees me" Genesis 16:11–14, Psalm 139:7–12—God knows our troubles.

JEHOVAH (JHVH-YHWH) "The self-existent one" Exodus 6:2–4, Psalm 102—One of the proper names of God. God never changes. He is faithful, and we need to obey Him. He is true and infinite. He is the Lord of all (Joel 2:32). The same Jehovah used in Joel 2:32 is the Jesus in Romans 10:11–13.

JEHOVAH JIREH "The Lord will provide" Psalm 23, Mark 10:45, Genesis 22:14—God provides all our needs. God provided His Son Jesus for our salvation. We must always trust that God will provide for us.

JEHOVAH SHALOM "The Lord our peace" Numbers 6:22–27, Hebrews 13:20, Judges 6:24—God Defeats our enemies. Jesus is the prince of peace. God gives us inner peace. Believers have peace through salvation (Colossians 1:19–20, Romans 5:1). We have been delivered from our rebellious ways to know God as our peace.

JEHOVAH ROHI "The Lord is my Shepherd" Psalm 23:1–3, John 10:14–18—The Lord protects leads, directs, and provides for His people. God takes care of us like a shepherd.

JEHOVAH RAPHA "The Lord who heals" Psalm 103:3, 1 Peter 2:24, Exodus 15:26—The Lord has provided healing for us spiritually and physically.

JEHOVAH SABAOTH "The Lord of armies (hosts)" Psalm 46:7, Romans 9:29—Even when people fail, the Lord will still fulfill His purposes.

JEHOVAH SHAMMAH "The Lord my companion is there" Ezekiel 48:35, Revelation 21—God is accessible to all who love Him. He is present with us. The Holy Spirit abides in all true believers who live in obedience.

JEHOVAH TSIDKENU "The Lord our righteousness" Jeremiah 23:5–6, 2 Corinthians 5:21—Jesus the King from the line of David imparts His Righteousness on us. As man, we are to recognize our sin. We are to confess that we are helpless and receive His promise (Romans 3:29).

JEHOVAH MEKADDISHKEM "The Lord who sanctifies" Exodus 31:12, Hebrews 13:12—We are set apart to God, a holy priesthood, our sins cleansed.

JEHOVAH-NISSI "The Lord is our banner" Exodus 17:8–16, Micah 7:8—The Lord keeps His people from destruction. He fights for them. As His children we should put on the full armor of God (Ephesians 6). The Lord is our refuge and strength (Psalm 46:1). He will not fail us. His banner over us is the love He has for us.

JEHOVAH RA-AH "The Lord our Shepherd" Psalm 23:1–6—David says our Shepherd is YHWH, the Lord Jesus Christ. Because he is our Shepherd, we are loved, have a new spiritual life, a sense of belonging, a purpose, and no fear of death. In Him, we are fully satisfied. As He leads us, we are divinely preserved and provided for. The Lord will guide His true sheep.

Chapter 5

Created Beings
Angels

As far as we know, God has created two types of beings; the first being the angels, and the second being mankind. Angels are less powerful than God and are inferior to God, and man is less powerful than angels. There is not much information about angels in the Bible. They are, however, seen in the Old and New Testaments in various places. The word "angel" means "messenger" or "one that is sent." Whether angels were created before the universe or after is unknown. The Bible does say they were created before mankind. They appear to be great in number, according to Scripture. Revelation 5:11says, *"Then I looked and I heard the voice of many angels around the throne and the living creatures and the elders; and the number of them was myriads of myriads, and thousands of thousands, saying with a loud voice, 'worthy is the lamb that was slain to receive power and riches and wisdom and might and honor and glory and blessing'"* (NIV).

The Bible says one third of the angels rebelled when they sided with Lucifer (an angel, now known as Satan and sometimes referred to as "the dragon" in Scripture) when he fell. *Then another sign appeared in heaven, and behold a great red dragon having seven heads and ten horns, and on his heads were seven diadems. And his tail swept away a third of the stars of heaven and threw them to the earth. And there was war in heaven, Michael and his angels waging war with the dragon. The dragon and his angels waged war and they were not strong enough, and there was no longer a place found for them in heaven* (Revelation 12:3–4, 7–8, NIV). We do know that the fallen angels with Satan are bent upon man's destruction and challenging God's sovereignty in spite of their sure end in the lake of fire. Jesus said that they steal, kill, and destroy. They also know there is only one God (James 2:19) and they tremble at the very name of Jesus

Angels were created holy and immortal to serve the Lord. They are spirits who can appear in human form to do God's will. Some were seen in the Bible with bright light around them, almost godlike in appearance, and some appeared quite large in size. They seem to have tremendous strength and superior intellect when compared to humans. Contrary to what some people think, when people die, they do not become angels.

1. In comparison to angels, what does Luke 20:34–36 say you will be like in God's future kingdom if you are counted worthy to be there?

_____

_____

_____

_____

2. What does 1 Corinthians 6:2–3 say is one of the things saints will be doing in the kingdom?

_____

_____

_____

_____

_____

There appears to be a ranking or order to angels in Scripture. Here is a list of the types of angels in the Bible:

Archangels—*For the Lord Himself will descend from heaven with a shout, with the voice of the archangel and with the trumpet of God* (1 Thessalonians 4:16, NASB).

Cherubim—*These are the living beings that I saw beneath the God of Israel by the river Chebar; so I knew that they were cherubim. Each one had four faces and each one four wings, and beneath their wings was a form of human hands. As for the likeness of their faces, they were the same faces whose appearance I had seen by the river Chebar. Each one went straight ahead* (Ezekiel 10:20–22, NASB).

Seraphim—*Then one of the seraphim flew to me with a burning coal in his hand which he had taken from the altar with tongs* (Isaiah 6:6, NASB).

Principalities, powers, and authorities of angels that have rank within rank and are either fallen (possibly demons) or elect (God's angels)—*So that the manifold wisdom of God might now be made known through the church to the rulers and the authorities in the heavenly places* (Ephesians 3:10, NASB). *For our struggle is not against flesh and blood, but against the rulers, against the powers,* *against the world forces of this darkness, against the spiritual forces of wickedness in the heavenly places* (Ephesians 6:12, NASB).

Angels serve God, and in many ways they protect believers (Matthew 18:10, Daniel 6:22, Psalm 91:1–16), particularly children. They worship God and perform His will (Revelation 5:11). They watch over churches (1Timothy 5:21) and minister to those who will inherit salvation (Hebrews 1:4–14). Angels will also help in spreading the gospel during the tribulation (Revelation 14:6–7). Angels, for the most part, do God's will undercover because seeing their splendor may cause man to worship them, and that is forbidden.

Thank God for those angels who stayed obedient to our Lord. We who are redeemed will forever stand with them to worship, exalt, and glorify our God. As for those people who are unredeemed, they have been aligned with the fallen angels, the devil, and are his captives in this world because of the fall. Their destination will ultimately be the lake of fire.

Man

What is man that you are mindful of Him, the son of man that you care for him? You made him a little lower than the heavenly beings and crowned him with glory and honor (Psalms 8:4–5, NIV).

There are many opinions of what man is. The one we hear of the most is that man evolved from lower life forms to what he is now. Another is that we are just a package of cells. One philosopher said we are a collection of accidental atoms, and that's it. But we all ask at one point or another, who am I? Why am I here? Why is man the way he is? Is a person's life just living a short while and then dying?

The first three chapters of Genesis tell us our origin. It tells how we are wonderfully made, yet flawed because of the fall—that man is not just a physical being, but also has a spirit and a soul. A soul with emotions and passions so that man can distinguish that he is alive. Man has spirit that allows him to reason, to know things, to distinguish that he is different from other animals, and to have personal communion with God. When a man dies, he is not an animal. His spirit goes back to God, and he will be judged for his life. If he has Jesus as Lord and Savior, he will be judged for what he did as a Christian. This is a time of rewards. True believers will be given eternal life with God and a new body. But people who do not have Jesus as Lord and Savior will be judged at the white throne judgment, resulting in a conscious eternal separation from God in the lake of fire. Man was made with free will to respond to God's love and to serve God. Man was created to glorify Him and live in His joy. 1 Thessalonians 5:23 says, *"Now may the God of peace Himself sanctify you entirely; and may your spirit and your soul and your body be preserved complete, without blame at the coming of our Lord Jesus Christ"* (NASB).

Man was created in God's image. God intentionally and personally created man. Man was no accident or product of evolution, but the ultimate culmination of all God had created. To God, man has worth. God's creation was spoken into existence by His power (let there be light, etc.). He said His creation was good. But when man was made, God was more personally involved (let

Us make man in Our image, Genesis1: 26–27, 2:7). Man was created a perfect being to reflect the nature of God. Mankind was created to love and have fellowship with God and other beings. When God was finished creating man, He said it was very good. All He had created, including man, was perfect. He put Adam and Eve over all creation on earth.

But something happened because Adam and Eve had the ability to choose, and they made a wrong choice. They were deceived and disobedient when they listened to Satan in the garden rather than trusting God. At that point, their connections with God were broken.

Separation from God, separation from others, separation from ourselves, and separation with nature were initiated because of sin and rebellion, which was spawned by the devil. Sin had caused man to be helpless, yet still of worth to God. God still loves man so much as to save him (John 3:16). Scripture is the story of God's love for man. It's a story where God reveals Himself to man and, by His love, restores the separations that occurred in the garden for those who respond to His call (John 17:1–26). He destroys the work of the devil and removes sin forever. He creates a new heaven and a new earth where we will forever be with Him. Where will you be?

3. You are created in God's image. How does that make you feel? What does it mean to be created in His Image?

_____

_____

_____

_____

Chapter 6

The Church

At the moment of a person's conversion, they become part of the Lord's one true church. The church is not a building. The Church includes all the true believers with Jesus as the head. Throughout history, Jesus has been working and living through His body of believers the church. The church shares the same purpose and mission by serving others and proclaiming the gospel.

The Lord's church is made up of many different people from around the world. These people are of different races, nations, cultures, and ages. Even though these people have never come together in one place, they meet in various places to worship the same one true God as one family, showing the world an example of the same love and selflessness as Jesus has (John 13: 12–17, Luke 22: 24–27). We take part in distributing God's compassion, for He has had compassion on us. What a privilege it is to be called as a church to display God's love and be used to help reconcile the lost to His kingdom.

Ephesians 1:9–10 says, *"He made known to us the mystery of His will, according to His kind intention which He purposed in Him with a view to an administration suitable to the fullness of the times, that is the summing up of all things in Christ, things in the heavens and things on earth"* (NASB).

You may have heard that a person does not need to meet with others as a church, but it is God's will that believers meet together. Hebrews 10:24–25 says, *"And let us consider how to stimulate one another to love and good deeds, not forsaking our own assembling together, as is the habit of some, but encouraging one another; and all the more as you see the day drawing near* (NASB). When we meet together, we have fellowship with other believers to worship and praise God. We hear and learn God's Word and learn what He wants for us as a church. When we fellowship together, we are being equipped for living in the world and ministry.

1. What does Revelation 21:3–4 say is the future state of God's Church?

_____

_____

_____

_____

Even though this is the wonderful future of the church, we are also His church now. The church currently is in a dark fallen world. Satan has lost the battle, and God is victorious over sin. He is in control. As the church, we are to be in the world and not of it. As the church, we are the light that shines in this dark, depraved world. We are a realm of subjects, imperfect as we may be in this world, with a perfect king. One day, we will exist as God's perfect church in His kingdom.

As the body of Christ, we must remember to keep our focus on Jesus as the head. If we fail to be led by His Spirit, we can become accustomed to routine as a church. We may become too structured and administrative. The Holy Spirit has to move when and where He wills, and we must follow as a church. If we allow Him, the Holy Spirit will move us with new ideas, outreach, and worship. The church is born of God, taken care of by God, and sustained by God as the following verses say:

You did not choose Me but I chose you, and appointed you that you would go and bear fruit, and that your fruit would remain, so that whatever you ask of the Father in My name He may give you (John15:16, NASB).

And God is able to make all grace abound to you, so that always having all sufficiency in everything, you may have abundance for every good deed; as it is written (2 Corinthians 9:8, NASB).

So *the church throughout all Judea and Galilee and Samaria enjoyed peace, being built up, and going on in the fear of the Lord and in the comfort of the Holy Spirit, it continued to increase* (Acts 9:31, NASB).

2. Why is Jesus the head of the church, according to Acts 20:28?

_____

_____

_____

_____

3. Where did believers of the early church meet and on what day of the week in1 Corinthians 16:19 and Acts 20:7?

_____

_____

_____

_____

4. What were they doing as the early church in Acts 2:42?

_____

_____

_____

_____

5. What does Paul say to Timothy about the church in 1 Timothy 4:6–8 and 11–13?

_____

_____

_____

_____

6. What does Jesus say about how we as the church should be in Matthew 5:13–16?

_____

_____

_____

7. Read the following verses and write down what God's purpose and will is for the church. Ephesians 3:10

_____

_____

2 Corinthians 5:18–20

_____

_____

Acts 1:8

_____

_____

1 Peter 2:9

_____

_____

How Do I Choose a Church Fellowship?

It is sometimes a problem choosing a church fellowship to attend. There are so many churches out there. How do I know which church is really preaching and teaching God's Word and following His will? There are so many and they appear to be okay; they have nice buildings, and the people are nice. This is my denomination—I have to go here. Their music and praise are what I like. The pastor is such a good speaker. They are so large—they must be all right. I won't have any accountability there. All my friends go there. I like the programs. I hear what I want to hear. They even say they are Christians and believe in Jesus. They make me feel good. I like what they believe.

Am I on the right path by choosing a particular church? The following four things should help you as the Holy Spirit leads you to the church fellowship He wants you to attend:

A. Before seeking the right church to regularly attend, you should sincerely pray for the Lord to lead you. How many of us are where the Lord wants us to be? How many of us are really letting the Holy Spirit lead us to where He wants us to be?

B. The church must have the Holy Bible as its ultimate final authority. Do they have expository teaching and preaching from God's Word? Do they trust and obey all God's Word and believe it to be true? *All Scripture is inspired by God and profitable for teaching, for reproof, for correction, for training in righteousness* (2 Timothy 3:16, NASB.)

C. The church must have true teachings and beliefs concerning the work and person of Jesus Christ. Does the church believe that Christ is the head of the Church and do they seek Him for guidance? A true church believes that all believers are part of the body of Christ. As a church, we welcome all believers.

D. Do they believe that Jesus is God and that He lived a sinless life? Do they believe He died for our sins on the cross, was buried, and rose again three days after the crucifixion? Do they believe He ascended into heaven and is seated at the right hand of the Father and that Jesus has all authority over heaven and earth? *For in Him all the fullness of Deity dwells in bodily form* (Colossians 2:9, NASB). *Which also you received, in which also you stand, by which also you are saved. Now I make known to you brethren, the gospel which I preached to you, if you hold fast the word which I preached to you, unless you believed in vain. For I delivered to you as of first importance what I also received, that*

Christ died for our sins according to the Scriptures, and that He was buried, and that He was raised on the third day according to the Scriptures (1 Corinthians 15:1–4, NASB). Does the church believe that salvation can only be obtained by faith in Jesus Christ? That we cannot do any work to gain salvation. We cannot add anything to the gospel but what is in the Scripture. There is no third testament. God has given the church the Old and New Testaments; that is more than enough for all of us. *I am amazed that you are so quickly deserting Him who called you by the grace of Christ, for a different gospel; which is really not another; only there are some who are disturbing you and want to distort the gospel of Christ. But even if we or an angel from heaven should preach to you a gospel contrary to what we have preached to you, he is to be accursed* (Galatians 1:6–9, NASB).

In Revelation chapters two and three, Jesus gave seven letters to seven churches concerning their condition. I recommend that you read these chapters for they will help you to recognize what Jesus wills for His church. These seven churches represent churches that existed during the first century after Christ's ascension and their characteristics. They also represent 2000 years of ages of church history, culminating with the Laodicean church, which exists just before and during the tribulation period.

These letters also show and reveal the condition that our hearts can be in. In each letter the Lord gives the churches a partial description of Himself. He also gives them approval of their works as a church. He talked about those issues He disapproves, and the judgment that will result. The Lord encourages change where it is needed and ends the letters with a promise for those who respond to His words. When reading these letters, one could ask questions about their own church and heart. The condemnations the Lord had for these churches are not so different from those we may see today in many fellowships. Following is what the Lord condemns them for:

Ephesus: They left their first love of God. They replaced it with routine formality, and ritualism.

Smyrna: No condemnation for this persecuted church.

Pergamum: A mix of church and state, a church too close to the world. Some were tangled in false teaching.

Thyatira: They had a problem with governmental and religious hierarchy, which caused them to compromise Christian values.

Sardis: A dead church in need of reformation to go back to their true calling.

Philadelphia: No condemnation for this evangelistic church with spiritual fervency.

Laodicea: A church turning from evangelistic zeal to a satisfied condition of lukewarmness and apostasy.

8. What are the promises Jesus gives to these churches if they overcome their issues?

_____

_____

_____

_____

Ephesus, Rev. 2:7

_____

_____

_____

_____

Smyrna, Rev. 2:11

_____

_____

_____

_____

Pergamum, Rev. 2:17

_____

_____

_____

_____

Thyatira, Rev. 2:26–29

_____

_____

_____

_____

Sardis, Rev. 3:5–6

_____

_____

_____

_____

Philadelphia, Rev. 3:12–13

_____

_____

_____

_____

Laodicea, Rev. 3:21–22

_____

_____

_____

_____

Because you have kept the word of My perseverance, I also will keep you from the hour of testing, that hour which is about to come upon the whole world, to test those who dwell on the earth. I am coming quickly; hold fast what you have, so that no one will take your crown (Revelation 3:10–11, NASB).

Chapter 7

Our Obedience

So whether you eat or drink or whatever you do, do it all for the glory of God (1Corinthians 10:31, NIV).

Is the God of heaven glorified by your life? We are called to love God with all of our being. Our Christian life is to glorify Him in all we do. With that comes our desire to obey because we love Him. *1Peter 1:14–16 says, "As obedient children do not conform to the evil desires you had when you lived in ignorance. But just as He who called you is holy, so be holy in all you do, for it is written: 'Be holy for I Am holy'"* (NIV). John 14:15 says, *"If you love Me, you will obey what I command"* (NIV). *1John 2:5 says, "But those who obey God's word really do love Him. That is the way to know whether or not we live in Him"* (NLT).

If we do not obey God, we show that we do not love Him as we should. Our continued disobedience indicates we are not walking in the truth. (1 John 4:6). God has laid down for our own protection guidelines to live by. They are to keep us from hurting ourselves. Without them, our sin and rebellion would lead us on the path of self-destruction. Man is his own worst enemy and can easily self-destruct. Christians should understand the evil of sin more than the world does, and they must recognize that sin is not only self-destructive, but is a refusal to accept God's authority. Christians should more fully understand the evil nature of man. Along with that, there will be times when Satan will accuse you and try to make you feel guilty of sin. His accusations are unfounded. He does this to destroy you. When you do sin, the Holy Spirit will convict you of it. Your only way out is to go to God in confession; this helps you to resist the Devil, and he will flee. When you do go to God for forgiveness, He forgives you, and you are released from it.

1. What does 1 John 2:3–4 say about those who are obedient?

_____

_____

_____

_____

2. What shows that a person will be in heaven for eternity, according to Matthew 7:21?

_____

_____

_____

_____

Trials and Temptation

James 1:2–4 says, *Consider it all joy, my brethren, when you encounter various trials. Knowing that the testing of your faith produces endurance. And let endurance have its perfect result, that you may be perfect and complete, lacking in nothing"* (NASV). All people experience suffering in their lives whether they are Christians or not. We have the privilege as Christians to count the trials of our lives as joy. As much as the world would ask, why count trials joy? The trials of life are unbearable and make me sad. They cause pain and are difficult to endure. Should I say that at least I am still alive or that I'm working up joyous feelings because it's not as bad as it appears? No, that is not why Christians can count it joy. We count it joy because we recognize God is working in our lives to strengthen our faith. Our joy is an attitude not a feeling.

In believers God uses trials and temptations for our benefit to mature and strengthen our faith. Satan uses them because he wants to hurt us and see us fail, rather than resist him.

3. What do trials do for believers, according to what you read in Romans 5:1–5?

_____

_____

_____

_____

4. Rather than murmuring and grumbling because of our suffering in trials, what should we do to help us understand our trials and view them from a godly perspective in the light of James 1:5–6?

_____

_____

_____

_____

5. What does James 1:12 say about those who endure under trials?

_____

_____

_____

_____

Our trials in life come from what we sow in the flesh and from Satan. They are used by God for our growth. They have a divine purpose—our holiness. We will not be tested beyond what we are able to handle (1 Cor. 10:13). It is important that we recognize God is with us in the trial and that He loves us. We should know that our faith will grow, and we will become more fruitful by our trials. For these reasons, we should have the attitude of joy in our trials. We should not complain about our circumstances but let the trial do what God wants for us.

We see the hand of God at work in our trials, and we have our focus on Him not ourselves. Our wrong attitude in the midst of trials can cause us to fall prey to sin because of temptations that can come in the trial. God will test our faith in a trial, but He will not tempt you with evil. On the other hand, Satan will tempt you to do evil and sin. We may even think the trial is unfair and blame God. We then grumble about our circumstances and are tempted to sin. *Let no one say when he is tempted, "I am being tempted by God," for God cannot be tempted, and He Himself does not tempt anyone* (James 1:13, NASB).

6. God does not tempt us (James 1:13). Where does temptation come from and where does it lead, according to James 1:14–16?

_____

_____

_____

_____

So we see by Scripture that we are tempted by our own desires and lusts. When we yield to our desires, we sin. When we sin it leads to death (the process of dying). What we need to do as believers is not sin. Expect temptation, which is not sin, to happen to you. Know that God will use it to test your faith. Also be aware that Satan will use it to try and get you to sin. Resist Satan and draw near to God. Do not let the temptation lead you to sin. Thomas Manton, the Puritan, said it this way in his Exposition on the Epistle of James: "It showeth what reason we have to mortify sin lest it mortify us; no sins are mortal but such as that are not mortified; either sin must die, or the sinner. The life of sin and the life of the sinner are like two buckets in a well; if the one goeth up then the other must come down. When sin liveth the sinner must die."

We are also given a warning in Scripture concerning temptation and sin in trials. In James 1:16, we are commanded not to be deceived. He says, "Don't be led astray." God is saying stop being fooled. Fooled by what? Letting our temptations fool us into sinning and taking them for granted. We then start to believe that we can just sin our lives to glory because we have God's grace. Yes, we are saved by His grace through Christ, and we can ask for forgiveness, but Scripture also says, *"For the grace of God has appeared, bringing salvation to all men, instructing us to deny all ungodliness and worldly desires and to live sensibly, righteously and godly in the present age. Looking for the blessed hope and the appearing of the glory of our great God and Savior, Jesus Christ; who gave Himself for us that He might redeem us from every lawless deed and purify for Himself a people for His own possession, zealous for good deeds"* (Titus 2:11–14, NASB).

Old Habits and Sin

In Ephesians, Paul says for a believer to put aside, or get rid of, those bad habits and sin that were a part of our "before Christ lifestyles." He says we are to do those things that lift us up and please the Lord. Ephesians 4:22–24 says, *You were taught with regard to your former way of life, to put off your old self, which is being corrupted by its deceitful desires, to be made new in the attitude of your minds; and to put on the new self, created to be like God in true righteousness and holiness"* (NIV)

7. What should we do, according to Ephesians 4:17?

_____

_____

_____

_____

8. List some of the ways you should live, according to Paul, as you continue to read Ephesians 4:25–5:21 in your Bible.

_____

_____

_____

_____

Putting off the old habits of sin is not as easy as it sounds. It is a life-long process and part of the Christian life; sins can be deep within us. Changing of habits and sin is a loving, conscious commitment to Jesus Christ. We do this knowing that what we will go through is not easy. Just as a person needs God in their life to replace all those worldly things, we need to replace our sin with something godly. So Paul says "put off" and "put on," which is to replace the old habits with godly ones. Don't just stop and leave an empty void. Replace the void. 2 Corinthians 7:1 says, *"Therefore, having these promises, beloved, let us cleanse ourselves from all defilement of flesh and spirit perfecting holiness in the fear of God"* (NASB).

9. According to 1 Thessalonians 5:21–22, what are we to do?

_____

_____

_____

_____

How can we tell what we should do or not? Is it okay to smoke, drink, watch TV, gamble, hang around with past friends, or do other forms of entertainment? Many sins are clearly mentioned in the Bible, but there are other areas that may be gray. If something is permitted in His Word then that is clear enough for us, and we can make heartfelt right decisions to live by. But if it is a sin, then why should I or should I not do it? This is a question of legalism or freedom that a true believer has. How does our obedience fit into that? After all, as Christians, we are free in Christ; all things are lawful. That tells me it is allowed, or is it? Is our obedience legalism? No, our obedience is not legalism. It is our love for the Lord that creates the freedom in us to want to obey.

Free in Christ

All things are lawful for me, but not all things are profitable. All things are lawful for me, but I will not be mastered by anything (1 Corinthians 6:12, NASB). Paul says that as a Christian he is free in Christ and is no longer judged by the Old Testament laws and regulations. Christians are saved by grace and, with this free gift of salvation, are no longer slaves to sin or the law. You may feel that sin or bad habits have power to hold you, but you have Jesus who has given you the freedom to deny and overcome them. Only by His grace and power you have victory, and you should believe it.

John 8:31–32 says, *"Jesus therefore was saying to those Jews who had believed Him, 'If you abide in my word, then you are truly disciples of Mine; and you shall know the truth and the truth shall make you free'"* (NASB).

Ephesians 2:10 says, *"For we are God's workmanship, created in Christ Jesus to do good works, which God prepared in advance for us to do"* (NASB).

When Jesus died for us on the cross, He paid our penalty for sin and freed us from it; therefore, sin has no power over us and we should not be preoccupied with it. When we try by our own power to keep rules and regulations to live by, we will eventually fail. When trying to keep rules by our own effort, we can become self-righteous and look down on others. We may even cause others to stumble in their walk. We are not perfect and will not be until we are with Him in glory. Yet, when we try to keep our own rules for ourselves, we begin a cycle that may lead to frustration and depression. We may, at this point, give up doing the things we should be doing like praying, reading the Word, and having fellowship with believers because we have made them rules and disciplines in our lives as we have tried with stopping our sin. My point is, by our efforts, we are setting ourselves up for failure and depression. This is a cycle you don't want to be in.

How, then, do we stop sinning and bad habits? How do we do those disciplines like fellowship, prayer, and being in the Word? After all, we are free in Christ, and we know that God does not like sin and wants us to live godly, blessed lives.

We do it by the love we have for God. Grace gives us freedom not to sin because we are no longer slaves to sin as the unsaved world is. The same goes for those gray areas like smoking, etc. There are no clear Scriptures concerning things like that, but 1 Corinthians 6:19 says that your body is the temple of the Holy Spirit, which is in you. You may have freedom to do these things, but you are not being very smart about it. These things will hurt you. They do not edify the Lord, and they may make someone who sees you do them stumble. When in doubt, avoid it. Ask yourself if it will enslave you. Will it hurt others, or cause them to stumble? Will it cause you to sin? Does it edify God? Is it helpful and will it hurt your body physically or spiritually?

Our obedience comes from our changed hearts and love for God, which motivates us to please our Lord. When we try to keep the laws, rules, and regulations, we get into the mindset Paul talks about in the following Scripture. *For the good that I wish, I do not do; but I practice the very evil that I do not wish. But if I am doing the very thing I do not wish, I am no longer the one doing it but sin which dwells in me. I find then the principle that evil is present in me, the one who wishes to do good. For I joyfully concur with the law of God in the inner man, but I see a different law in the members of my body, waging war against the law of my mind, and making me a prisoner of the law of sin which is in my members. Wretched man that I am! Who will set me free from the body of this death?* (Romans 7:19–24, NASB).

We should have the mindset that we know all things are lawful for the true believer but not all things are going to glorify God or benefit me. I will not be a slave to any habit or sin because Christ freed me from them. I will obey Him because I love Him and His ways. I want to glorify my Lord.

I will not win His love by my attempts at perfection. He already loves me. I do not have to live an up and down walk with Him from self-righteousness to failure by trying to keep rules.

How God Wants Us to Live

With our freedom in Christ and our love for Him in mind, we will now look at how God wants us to live. Our Lord wants us to be pure and holy. Jesus said in Matthew 5:27–28 that even our impure thoughts are sin, just as the action would be. He compared anger to murder and adulterous thoughts to adultery as examples. Therefore, Scripture tells us not to think of sinful behaviors.

10. Read Philippians 4:8–9 and write down the things we are to think about instead of impure thoughts.

_____

_____

_____

_____

What will happen when you do this?

_____

_____

_____

_____

11. According to Romans 8:7, what keeps people from thinking pure thoughts?

_____

_____

_____

12. How do we overcome sinful thoughts?

_____

_____

_____

_____

13. What are some of the things you may need to avoid to live in the Spirit and keep from thinking impure thoughts?

_____

_____

_____

_____

Remember that the Lord is a forgiving God. When we sin, we can repent of it and ask Him to forgive us. 1 John 1:9 says, *"If we confess our sins, He is faithful and just and will forgive us our sins and purify us from all unrighteousness"* (NIV). 1 Corinthians 10:13 says, *"No temptation has seized you except what is common to man. And God is faithful He will not let you be tempted beyond what you can bear. But when you are tempted, He will also provide a way out so that you can stand up under it"* (NIV).

14. List some of the blessings that come with obedience according to the following verses.

John 15:10

_____

_____

_____

_____

John 15:14

_____

_____

_____

_____

1 John 3:22

_____

_____

_____

_____

Pray that God gives you a love for Him that surpasses everything and everyone you are acquainted with and that you have a great desire to obey Him in all ways.

Baptism

Matthew 28:19 says, *"Therefore go and make disciples of all the nations, baptizing them in the name of the Father and the Son and the Holy Spirit"* (NIV). Baptism is one of the first acts of obedience Jesus wants us to do when we are saved. In baptism, we are identified with Jesus Christ by His death, burial, and resurrection. By our baptism, we show the church and the world who are and claim to be in Christ. Baptism is not an ordinance we do to be saved as some believe. That would be works for salvation. We are saved by grace through faith. It is a gift from God. Belief comes first and baptism comes after. That is what it says in Scripture. Those that have confessed Jesus as Lord should be baptized. *They replied, "Believe in the Lord Jesus and you will be saved, along with your entire household." Then they shared the word of the Lord with him and all who lived in his household. That same hour the jailer washed their wounds, and he and everyone in his household were immediately baptized.* (Acts 16:31–33, NIV).

15. If you have confessed Jesus as your Lord, have you also been baptized?

_____

_____

_____

_____

16. What does the picture portrayed in Romans 6:3–5 signify to the believer?

_____

_____

_____

_____

God now sees us in Jesus. We are dead to sin and God does not see us as sinners, but as people that that have resurrection life in His kingdom. Galatians 2:20 says, *"I have been crucified with Christ and I no longer live, but Christ lives in me. The life I live in the body, I live by faith in the son of God who loved me and gave Himself for me"* (NIV).

The Lord's Supper

The Lord's Supper, or communion, is another church ordinance Jesus asked us to observe. It is done as an act of remembering what Christ did for us by going to the cross. *For this is what the*

Lord Himself said, and I pass it on to you just as I received it. On the night that He was betrayed the Lord Jesus took a loaf of bread, and when He had given thanks, He broke it and said, "This is My body, which is given for you. Do this in remembrance of Me." In the same way He took a cup of wine after supper, saying, "This cup is the new covenant between God and you, sealed by the shedding of My blood. Do this in remembrance of me as often as you drink it." For every time you eat this bread and drink this cup, you are announcing the Lord's death until He comes again (1 Corinthians 11:23–26, NLT).

Living by Faith

Christian's are to live by faith. Faith is how a Christian is to live and function. Faith is the knowledge, trust, and action towards an object we choose to believe to be true. Faith always needs an object. With Christians, the object we have faith in is God. Jesus is the object of faith, and He never changes (Hebrew 13:8). We have the confidence and trust that what God says he will do and so we act upon it. Our faith grows as we hear God's Word (the gospel) and His truth. As we see God work through the circumstances in our lives, our relationships with God increase and our faith in Jesus becomes stronger. Even our salvation is based on faith. A person cannot be saved without faith. Ephesians 2:8–9 says, *"For it is by grace you have been saved through faith and this not from yourselves, it is the gift of God, not by works, so that no one can boast"* (NASB).

From that Scripture, we see that faith is a gift from God, so we see those that do not have faith in God (the world) and those that do (Christians). God gives us the faith to believe Him.

17. How does a person receive faith, according to Romans 10:17?

_____

_____

_____

_____

18. What is the true object of our faith, according to Acts 20:21?

_____

_____

_____

_____

19. What action of faith should you take with your life, showing that you really have faith in Christ?

_____

_____

_____

_____

Chapter 8

Spiritual Gifts and Ministry

Christians and members of Christ's body, the Church, must have a desire to worship and serve the Lord. The Holy Spirit gives to each Christian spiritual gifts for use in ministry to build up the body. 1 Corinthians 12:4–6 says, *"Now there are different kinds of spiritual gifts, but it is the same Holy Spirit who is the source of them all. There are different kinds of service in the church, but it is the same Lord we are serving. There are different ways God works in our lives, but it is the same God who does the work through all of us"* (NLT). By the verses we see that there are varieties of gifts, services, and workings.

1. How should we use our spiritual gifts, according to 1 Peter 4:10–11?

_____

_____

_____

_____

    The gifts we have been given all have different functions. We can demonstrate and show love to others by the use of our gifts for others. Christians should be drawn with a burden to do some kind of service in the body. You may have a desire to do something in your local church or to work with kids. You may want to work with youth or adults. Where are your compassions leaning? Do you see brokenness in particular areas in this world that you feel drawn to help in?

    When you find that area that you want to serve in, people will be built up because God will use your gifts to glorify Himself.

2. What does Romans 12:6–8 say about how we should allow people in the church to use their spiritual gifts?

_____

_____

_____

_____

3. How can a person's spiritual gifts be used in the wrong manner, according to 1 Corinthians 13:1–3?

_____

_____

_____

_____

4. How is love described in context to our using spiritual gifts?

_____

_____

_____

_____

5. Besides in love, how are we to minister and exercise our spiritual gifts for others, according to the following verses?

2 Corinthians 5:7

_____

_____

James 1:5

_____

_____

_____

_____

1 Corinthians 12:25

_____

_____

_____

_____

Hebrews 10:23–24

_____

_____

_____

_____

2 Timothy 2:15

_____

_____

_____

_____

2 Corinthians 9:7

_____

_____

_____

_____

6. How does the church grow, according to Eph. 4:11–16?

_____

_____

_____

_____

Although there is no set formula for knowing what your gifts are, there are ways you can discover them. First you should try to live a life of obedience, and use the answers to questions four and five. The leaders in your church can help you by equipping you for the use of spiritual gifts. Others that know you will also be able to see the areas that you may be gifted in. Another way is to consider whether you like what you are doing. Do you have a feeling of gratification and fulfillment when you exercise or try a gift? Following is a list of most of the spiritual gifts. You may discover after reading them that these are some you would like to try.

Miracles are bringing glory to God by supernatural acts that go beyond natural laws and prove the servant of God to be authentic.

Tongues are speaking a language unknown to the speaker. This is spoken only to God and is to be accompanied by someone's gift of interpretation.

Healing is intervening through faith and prayer in the curing of someone's illness.

Knowledge is wisdom and understanding of Scripture as a revelation from God or acquired through scholarship.

Wisdom is applying insight through the Holy Spirit to meet specific needs.

Discernment is recognizing the difference between truth and error—whether something is from God, Satan, or man.

Administration is leadership ability to make decisions that help oversee the church.

Exhortation is the ability to encourage, motivate, or rebuke a person, with love, for deeper spiritual commitment and action.

Giving is giving to others with joy in response to their needs.

Mercy is showing compassion, meeting others' needs whether physical, emotional, or spiritual.

Helps are bearing one another's burdens, serving with or for them.

Hospitality is serving with joy in your home or church.

Service is meeting the material needs of others by performing tasks that benefit others.

Evangelism is a passion to let others know the grace of God by proclaiming the gospel and by your life.

Teaching is communicating to others God's truths for life transformation.

7. Which gifts do you see that you have, would like to be trained for, or would like to try?

_____

_____

_____

_____

Ask God to help you with direction on what area you should minister in. Ask others and the leaders of your church to help guild you. You are called to be involved to build up the body and bring glory to God.

Chapter 9

Prayer

In our Christian life, we communicate with God by prayer. Prayer is a two-way link of communication between God and us. It is a means of cultivating a relationship and friendship with Him. Our spiritual maturity grows in prayer and our quiet time with God. We are commanded to pray in Scripture. 1 Timothy 2:8 says, *"I want men everywhere to lift up holy hands in prayer, without anger or disputing"* (NIV). 1 Thessalonians 5:17–18 says, *"Pray continually, give thanks in all circumstances, for this is God's will for you in Christ Jesus"* (NIV). Ephesians 6:18 says, *"And pray in the Spirit on all occasions with all kinds of prayers and requests. With this in mind, be alert and always keep on praying for the saints"* (NIV).

1. Read Hebrews 13:15. What does it say we are to do?

_____

_____

_____

_____

In these Scriptures, we see that our praying should be continual. In prayer, we worship God, praise God, and give thanks to God. We should pray in times of trouble, when others need help, and for our needs. Pray for His protection and for wisdom in applying the armor of God (Ephesians 6:10–18). We should pray for our pastors, missionaries, those serving the Lord, and the Church. Pray for the salvation of your unsaved friends and relatives. Pray for those who are sick and for our country. We should also pray to be guided by and to be continually filled with the Holy Spirit. Pray for our enemies. Above all, we should pray that God is glorified in all things including the answers to our prayers.

However, because of man's fall and depravity, we do not pursue prayer, and we think it is difficult. We see prayer as a last resort to get out of tough situations. We fight against our flesh, our sin, and the devil, which keeps us from praying. We have problems focusing, concentrating, and speaking what needs to be said in prayer. When we do pray, it is for something we want from God, not realizing that prayer is God's way of giving us what He wants. Still, the Lord said that Christians should pray continually. Other than a prayer for salvation, only redeemed people of God, those saved through Jesus, can do this and know He not only hears, He answers. Jesus gives us a personal invitation to have communion with Him, and like most of the things of God concerning man, He takes the initiative. Revelation 3:20 says, *"Behold I stand at the door and knock; if anyone hears my voice and opens the door, I will come in to him and dine with him, and he with Me"* (NASB).

Jesus also taught His disciples about prayer. Luke 18:1 says, *"Then Jesus told His disciples a parable to show them that they should always pray and not give up"* (NIV). We will look at Jesus' model for prayer later in this chapter.

2. According to James 5:13–16, what kinds of prayer can a righteous person expect answers to through faith?

_____

_____

_____

_____

3. Read the following Scriptures and write down some of the purposes of prayer.

1 John 1:9

_____

_____

_____

_____

James 1:5

_____

_____

_____

_____

Matthew 26:41

_____

_____

_____

_____

Colossians 1:9–12

_____

_____

_____

_____

1 Thessalonians 5:17–18

_____

_____

_____

_____

4. Although we may choose any time of the day to have a quiet time and prayer with God, why might it be best to have your quiet time early in the morning?

_____

_____

_____

_____

5. According to Mark 1:35, when did Jesus choose to spend time alone in prayer with the Father?

_____

_____

_____

_____

It is best to have a consistent time and place to spend in the Word and in prayer with God. In these times, God instructs and guides us through His Word. We can think up many excuses for why not to pray. The most used reason we have is that we have no time. But when you really think about it, do we have less time than Jesus had? Yet, He still managed to find time to spend with the Father.

6. In Luke 10:38–42, Jesus deals with the very issue of our time. What is the difference between what Martha made the time for and what Mary made time for?

_____

_____

_____

_____

To have a relationship with someone, we have to spend time with him or her. The more time you spend with God, the stronger your relationship will become. Satan does not want us to pray because our relationship grows as we spend time with God. Satan also does not want us to know the power of prayer. We need to remember that Satan has a strategy to keep us from praying. The devil hates prayer.

7. How might Satan try to distract you from praying?

_____

_____

_____

_____

How might Satan try to discourage you from praying?

_____

_____

_____

_____

How might Satan try to disqualify you from praying?

_____

_____

_____

_____

Conditions for Answered Prayer

First, we must be saved, and then we must obey Jesus' commands. John 15:7 says, *"If you abide in Me, and My words abide in you, ask whatever you wish, and it shall be done for you."*

8. In your Bible, turn to 1 John 3:22 and write, in your own words, what it says.

_____

_____

_____

_____

Second we must pray and ask with the right motives. We should have our will aligned with God's. To know the Lord's will in most instances is to simply go to the Word of God. Does our prayer line up with Scripture? James 4:2–3 says, *"You want what you don't have, so you scheme and kill to get it. You are jealous for what others have, and you can't possess it, so you fight and quarrel to take it away from them. And yet the reason you don't have is that you don't ask God for it. And even when you do ask, you don't get it because your whole motive is wrong, you want only what will give you pleasure"* (NLT).

Third, when we pray we should be totally focused upon God and not pray to be seen by others. Yes, we pray together, and we should pray separately. In the Bible, there are times when we see people praying together and out loud. What we should not do is pray to be seen by others, as if we are praying to be heard and seen by others. God does not care how articulate we are or how spiritual we appear to others in prayer. He wants our hearts. When we seek to be seen or heard by others, it is hypocrisy. When we concern ourselves on what others might be thinking of our eloquence in group prayer, we lose focus. This can also discourage others from praying. When we pray that way, are we really sincere?

9. What does Jesus say about prayer in Matthew 6:5–6?

_____

_____

_____

_____

Psalm 91:1says, *"He who dwells in the shelter of the Most High will rest in the shadow of the Almighty"* (NASB). God is self-sufficient. He does not need anything; there is nothing He cannot do. Yet, He has provided prayer as the means and privilege for Christians to communicate with Him and come alongside Him to accomplish His will. Our conversation with God should be as if we were talking to Him. When we pray, it should not be with repetitive or monologue language. When Jesus was on this earth, He prayed to the Father with plain conversation. So should we. We should be drawn to Him with a sense of need and faith, speaking to Him from our hearts. Psalm 27:8 says, *"My heart says to you, 'Seek His face!' Your face Lord, I will seek"* (NIV). Ecclesiastes 5:2 says, *"Do not be hasty in word or impulsive in thought to bring up a matter in the presence of God. For God is in heaven and you are on earth; therefore let your words be few"* (NASB).

10. What is your understanding of Matthew 6:7–8?

_____

_____

_____

_____

Remember that we serve a prayer-answering God with whom we have a personal relationship. He wants the best for us. Sometimes what we ask for is not what we need. God gives us what we need. When it seems that He is not answering your prayers, trust Him and wait in faith, trusting that He will respond in the best way. The Lord either has something better for you or wants you to learn something while you wait. Praying with a lack of forgiveness in your heart for those who have offended you or sin not confessed will also hinder your prayer life.

11. Paul, in 2 Corinthians 12:8–9, talks about a prayer he made to God three times. How did God respond to Paul's request?

_____

_____

_____

_____

_____

The Model Prayer

In Matthew 6:9–13 Jesus' disciples asked Him to teach them how to pray. They saw the relationship Jesus had with the Father and that He went to spend time with Him morning and night. Jesus then gave them a model or pattern for prayer in the following verses:

Our Father in heaven, hallowed be your name, your kingdom come, your will be done on earth as it is in heaven. Give us today our daily bread. Forgive us our debts, as we also have forgiven our debtors. And lead us not into temptation, but deliver us from the evil one (Matthew 6:9–13, NKJV).

Our Father in heaven—we are addressing God the Father in our prayers. As true believers, we have the right to call Him Father. This is possible because of our relationship and who we are in Jesus Christ, who is the Father's only begotten Son. It implies a personal relationship between child and Father. By faith we profess to be His children. It is a relationship where the Father loves and protects His child. The child also loves the Father, although the Father initiates this mutual love. We do not pray to angels or other saints. Jesus said to pray to His Father in His name.

Hallowed be your name—the Father, His Name, His attributes are holy and set apart from all. He should be treated that way when we pray. He is sovereign in the heavens and on earth, which He created. His attributes are beyond our comprehension. He is the Father of our Lord and Savior Jesus Christ. He is to be glorified in all prayer, especially for His attributes, which includes His mercy, forgiveness, power, truth, and justice. Even Jesus prayed in John 12:28, "Father, glorify your name." We approach God with reverence and respect when we pray. We don't start swinging away with our agenda when we pray.

Your kingdom come—we should pray for God's eternal kingdom to come in its fullness. God's kingdom will one day be manifested fully in every way. This kingdom will have no sin or evil in it.

Your will be done on earth as it is in heaven—His will is being done in heaven, and we should pray that it will be done on earth as well. This will come with His final kingdom. As Christians, we should try to live it now. Pray that mankind on earth will obey as the angels in heaven. That we know His will, obey it, and submit to it. The secret to effective prayer is to focus on God, His will, and His kingdom first. Not what you need and want. He knows what we need. He will hear you when you ask. Jesus said in Matthew 6:33 for us to seek first the kingdom of God and the things we need will be added.

Give us today our daily bread —at this point, we should pray for the necessities we require. All these things come from His abundant blessings. We should acknowledge our total dependence upon God. Be thankful in prayer for what He provides and what you have. Be specific when you ask. As James said, "You have not because you ask not." God is concerned even with the small needs of life.

Forgive us our debts as we have forgiven our debtors —we need daily confession and forgiveness for our sins. We see in this verse that God will forgive us when we are willing to forgive others. This shows that we have repentant hearts. If God is willing to forgive our sin, we should be willing to forgive those who sin against us. When we do not forgive, we have not experienced God's forgiveness and realized the depth of His forgiveness for us. Remember that we may feel undeserving of forgiveness, and so may those that we need to forgive. Forgive those who have sinned against you. A believer should ask forgiveness of sin on a daily basis. Sin will hinder your devotional time with God. Sin will make approaching God more difficult as you wait to confess it. Do it right away. Be honest and sincere; be contrite and confess with a repentant heart. Have faith in knowing He will forgive you.

And lead us not into temptation, but deliver us from the evil one —pray for deliverance and protection from the devil's attacks. His attacks are to get us to sin and fail morally. He does this through temptation. Pray that you are delivered from the temptations and the resulting sins in your life.

12. In the space below, write a prayer out in your own words, using the model Jesus said to use in Matthew 6: 9–13.

_____

_____

_____

_____

He who has My commandments and keeps them is the one who loves Me; and he who loves Me will be loved by My Father, and I will love him and will disclose Myself to him. Jesus answered and said to him, If anyone loves Me, he will keep My word; and My Father will love him, and We will come to him and make Our abode with him" (John 14:21,23, NASB). *Delight yourself in the Lord and He will give you the desires of your heart* (Psalm 37:4, NKJV).

Fasting

When you fast do not look somber as the hypocrites do, for they disfigure their faces to show men they are fasting. I tell you the truth, they have received their reward in full. But when you fast put oil on your head and wash your face, so that it will not be obvious to men that you are fasting, but only to your Father, who is unseen; and your Father, who sees what is done in secret, will reward you (Matthew 6:16–18, NIV).

Fasting is something that Christians should do, although it is not practiced enough today. Jesus, when He spoke to His disciples in Matthew 6:16–18, said *when* you fast, not if you fast. So, it was assumed fasting was part of their everyday life. People fast for many reasons such as health, weight, and penitence reasons. These reasons are not what God intended as fasting. Our fasting, like other prayer habits, is to be from the heart and sincere. It is done with God in focus. Our fasting and prayer is not usually shared with others, unless for specific reasons. Fasting and prayer must go together because it is spiritual. There are many places in the Bible where fasting was done.

13. Write out some of the reasons people in the OT and NT fasted.

Moses in Deuteronomy 9:18–19

_____

_____

_____

_____

David in 1 Samuel 1:11–12

_____

_____

_____

_____

Jesus in Luke 4:1

_____

_____

_____

Anna in Luke 2:36–38

_____

_____

_____

Fasting in a biblical sense is in most instances abstinence from food for a designated period of time, and it is done for spiritual reasons. It may be to abstain from just food or food and water. Fasting can also be to abstain from other things such as a particular thing in life (TV, radio, work, or sexual relations with your spouse) for a period of time, but it should always be for spiritual reasons with a focus on prayer and God. You will find that fasting is a spiritual discipline that produces great results such as a self-realized renewing of your relationship with God.

14. Read Isaiah 58:1–11 and write down next to the verses below what the prophet said about the discipline of fasting.

Isaiah 58:4

_____

_____

_____

Isaiah 58:5

_____

_____

_____

Isaiah 58:6

_____

_____

_____

Isaiah 58:7

_____

_____

_____

Isaiah 58:8

_____

_____

_____

_____

Isaiah 58:9

_____

_____

_____

_____

As you can see, there is a spiritual benefit to fasting. Just make sure it is done without calling attention to others and keep your focus on God. Make sure your motives are pure. Do it before God and not before men, not to earn God's favor, but to seek God. By this, you will see spiritual results.

Quiet Time with God

Do you have regular devotional time with the Lord? How much time do you spend with God every day? If we spend no time or little time with the Lord, we don't grow to know Him intimately. What we accomplish for God may only be fleshly endeavors. We should be serious about our devotional time with God and discipline ourselves to develop the quality time we spend with Him. Not by way of training the flesh, but by being humbled and knowing it is what God desires of His children. Devotional time with God is not something that is rushed, but it is done knowing that God is present with us. In this time, our focus is totally on God. It is so we will grow in knowing Him. John 17:3 says, "*This is eternal life that they may know You, the only true God, and Jesus Christ whom You have sent*" (NASB).

It starts with the fear of God, which seems to be diminishing in people as the times go on. Ask yourself: Do I really fear God? Do I know what it means to fear God? He created everything, is Holy, is superior in worth and dignity. He alone is God and is sovereign over His creation and yet wants me to be in relationship with Him.

And they sang the song of Moses, the bond-servant of God, and the song of the Lamb, saying, "Great and marvelous are your works, O Lord God, the Almighty: Righteous and true are Your ways, King of the nations! Who will not fear, O Lord, and glorify Your name? For You alone are holy; for all the nations will come and worship before You. For Your righteous acts have been revealed" (Revelation 15:3–4, NASB).

Do you not fear Me?' declares the Lord. Do you not tremble in My presence? For I have placed the sand as a boundary for the sea, an eternal decree, so it cannot cross over it. Though the waves toss, yet they cannot prevail; though they roar yet they cannot cross over it. But this people have a stubborn and rebellious heart; they have turned aside and departed. They do not say in their heart, "Let us now fear the Lord our God, who gives rain in its season, both the autumn rain and the spring rain, who keeps for us the appointed weeks of the harvest" (Jeremiah 5:22–24, NKJV).

For the unbeliever there is no fear of God. This means guilt and judgment, whether they believe it or not. For a Christian, it is a deterrent to sin as well as a growing love for God that helps us see God with respect, reverence, and awe. This alone is enough to encourage us to praise and worship Him. To fear God is to be truly spiritual. Fearing God is a characteristic that shows we are in true fellowship with Him and that we are part of His family. The measure of growth in a Christian's life as well as the life of a church is in proportion to their fear of God. It is where our holiness in life starts and grows from. 2 Corinthians 7:1 says, *"Therefore, having these promises, beloved, let us cleanse ourselves from all defilement of flesh and spirit, perfecting holiness in the fear of God"* (NASB).

15. What happened to the church in Acts 9:31 when they lived in the fear of the Lord?

_____

_____

16. In Deuteronomy 6:24, why are we commanded to fear God?

_____

_____

_____

In Jeremiah 10:6-7?

_____

_____

_____

_____

17. According to Proverbs 9:10, the fear of the Lord is the beginning of what?

_____

_____

_____

_____

18. What are some of the ways that God will bless those who fear Him in the following verses?

Psalm 103:11–17

_____

_____

_____

_____

Psalm 33:18–19

_____

_____

_____

_____

Ecclesiastes 8:12–13

_____

_____

_____

_____

Proverbs 14:26–27

_____

_____

_____

_____

19. Solomon, the wisest man that ever lived, tried to find satisfaction in the things and the pleasures of life. After he had tried everything and found everything unfulfilling, what was his final decision concerning life?

_____

_____

_____

_____

In our daily quiet time with God, we should spend time with His Word. When we do, we should not just read it, but expect to meet with the Lord. Expect to hear from Him as you pray, worship, and read His Word. Joshua 1:8 says, "*This book of the Law shall not depart from your mouth, but you shall meditate in it day and night, that you may observe to do all that is written in it. For then you will make your way prosperous, and then you will have good success*" (NASB).

The Lord is pleased when we spend time with Him. We were created to have intimate fellowship with God. As true believers, saved by the blood of Jesus, we are now able to do so. What a wonderful privilege. *And the life was manifested, and we have seen and testify and proclaim to you the eternal life which was with the Father and was manifested to us, what we have seen and heard we proclaim to you also so that you to may have fellowship with us, and indeed our fellowship is with the Father and His Son Jesus Christ* (1 John 1: 2-3, NASB). *But the Hour is coming, and now is, when the true worshipers will worship the Father in spirit and truth, for the Father is seeking such to worship Him* (John 4:23, NASB).

We tend to think that our time in prayer and meditation is only for ourselves. It is our nature. But we should think that it is for God as well. We know what desires we have on our hearts, and so does the Lord. That does not mean we should not ask, but remember to ask what the Lord is getting out of this time with you. Are you praising Him? Are you thankful? Are you glorifying Him? What is the Lord saying to you in your time with Him? Remember, it is a two-way communication, a relationship, and you will get much out of your time with the Lord. You will learn from Him. You will grow in your relationship with Him. He will encourage you as you grow and mature as a Christian.

What do I need to do to have more consistent and effective prayer and time with God? Check the ones you believe will help you.

___Get up earlier in the morning
___Spend less time with friends, TV, hobbies, etc.
___Discipline myself
___Ask God for help
___Find a place to do it
___Other

I have decided to try and spend quiet time with the Lord at _____ AM or PM every day. I will use this time to be in the Word, in prayer, and personal worship. I expect to receive from the Lord during this time. I know God will meet my spiritual needs and hear my prayers.

Signed _____

Pray that God helps you to see His will in your prayers. Pray that your will is aligned with His will and that your motives are sincere. Ask God to help you to have a great desire and faith to pray continually and spend quiet time with Him. To have true prayer and exclude everything that might hinder it. Ask God to help you remember that in prayer you have entered a holy place where God is. Ask him to help you with your words and tell Him you understand that He already knows your needs. Ask Him to answer what He determines is best. May He be glorified.

Chapter 10

False Beliefs

False teaching on the truths about God has existed since the beginning of man. God, eternal existence, salvation, man's purpose, and life in general have all been attacked. For mankind, it starts in Genesis where the devil gets man to disobey and fall by lying to him. This gave the devil the ruler-ship of the world until his defeat at the cross.

The Devil Behind It All

Before moving on with false teaching, we need to know its origin so we will talk about the devil and his angels (demons) first. They exist in the spiritual realms. The Bible says that the devil's original name was Lucifer. It says God created him perfect. It appears he was a high-ranking angel in the heavenly host (all angels). When Satan fell, he persuaded one third of all the angels created to side with him. Some are free to do Satan's bidding, and some are imprisoned for judgment.

1. What does Jesus say about the devil in Luke 10:18?

_____

_____

_____

_____

And the angels who did not keep their own domain, but abandoned their proper abode, He has kept in eternal bonds under darkness for the judgment of the great day (Jude 6, NASB).

How you have fallen from heaven, O star of the morning, son of the dawn! You have been cut down to the earth, you who have weakened the nations! But you said in your heart, "I will ascend to heaven; I will raise my throne above the stars of God, and I will sit on the mount of assembly in the recesses of the north. I will ascend above the heights of the clouds; I will make myself like the Most High" (Isaiah 14:12–14, NASB).

Again the word of the Lord came to me saying, "Son of man, take up a lamentation over the king of Tyre and say to him, Thus says the Lord God, "You had the seal of perfection, Full of wisdom and perfect in beauty. You were in Eden, the garden of God; Every precious stone was your covering: The ruby, the topaz and the diamond; the beryl, the onyx and the jasper; the lapis lazuli, the turquoise and the emerald; and the gold, the workmanship of your settings and sockets, Was in you. On the day that you were created they were prepared. You were the anointed cherub who covers, and I placed you there. You were on the holy mountain of God; you walked in the midst of the stones of fire. You were blameless in your ways from the day you were created until unrighteousness was found in you. By the abundance of your trade you were internally filled with violence, and you sinned; therefore I have cast you as profane from the mountain of God. And I have destroyed you, O covering cherub, from the midst of the stones of fire. Your heart was lifted up because of your beauty; you corrupted your wisdom by reason of your splendor. I cast you to the ground; I put you before kings, that they may see you. By the multitude of your iniquities, in the unrighteousness of your trade you profaned your sanctuaries. Therefore I have brought fire from the midst of you; it has consumed you, and I have turned you to ashes on the earth in the eyes of all who see you. All who know you among the peoples are appalled at you; you have become terrified and you will cease to be forever" (Ezekiel 28:11–19, NASB)

Satan was defeated at the cross and will ultimately be cast into the lake of fire with his angels (demons). But before he does, he will manipulate the godless of this world into a one-world government. They will unknowingly help him to be in power. This evil world empire is the culmination of what the devil has been working to accomplish through the ages. In these last days, those that become Christians who are alive at this time will be persecuted, most unto death (Rev.6:9–11). Satan will have a world religion composed of the many false beliefs, including some lukewarm churches we see today.

Today, we already see some churches beginning to tolerate sin with their leadership and congregations, those things the Bible tells us not to tolerate. As true believers, we must be prepared by putting on the full armor of God (Ephesians 6:10–18). Scripture says hell was created by God for the ultimate judgment of Satan and his angels. Those people who have rejected the free gift of salvation will be cast into the lake of fire as well. God created all things, and they all belong to him. He will not let those who don't want to be in his kingdom exist in his creation. They will be set apart for eternity.

Satan, for now, is allowed to usurp the world as he reigns until he is finally cast into the abyss and ultimately into the lake of fire. Satan attacks Jesus' Church in all sorts of ways. Because of him, we live in a fast-becoming godless society. This is sure sign that our Lord is coming very soon to remove all true Christians before God's wrath comes upon this world. That is why there is so much false teaching. Satan knows that man is the apple of God's eye. We are created in his image to glorify God. There is a tremendous eternity for those of us that are saved that we cannot even begin to comprehend.

Some of Satan's influences throughout history are from those evils we see in plain view such as: killing, sexual perversion, greed, lust, pride, power, and schools that teach evolution theories without regard for teaching the truth of intelligent design. The perversions of science are accepted rather than seeing proofs of God's existence in science. Political views that promote hoarding riches, alternate lifestyles, abortion, etc.—these are clearly against what God says in the Bible, yet Satan uses them all.

The devil has another weapon, and it is subtle. He would rather have a person not believe that he or God exists. The job is done. It is easy to lead a person who does not believe in him or God to conscious eternal damnation.

Satan's Many Lies

Satan also uses religions and different belief systems to lead people astray. He uses Satanism, witchcraft, and religions such as Hinduism and Buddhism. He uses spiritualism, pluralism, and New Age philosophies such as post modernism, etc. He uses them all—whatever will attract a person or group away from the real truth of the gospel. He copies and perverts true beliefs so that most will fall prey to one. He causes people to blame the problems of the world on man's religions to lead them into atheism. He does this to destroy man and hurt God.

Studying pagan religions can carry a danger that we should understand. Some people try to say truths of the Bible really originated from pagan religions. This is a ploy from Satan, who is a great imitator. If he can get you to believe that the truths of the Bible are from other early religions, he has won a battle. A good example is an early Persian religion called Zoroastrianism, where some beliefs appear to be the same as what is written in the Bible. When you study the religion, it can become confusing until after further study you find that it is believed Zoroaster was an Israelite from the lost tribes and was actually influenced by the Hebrew writings.

Nietzsche, a German philosopher, wrote his own beliefs on Zoroastrianism and added his own ideas to it. Here we see the compounding of false beliefs even further, which results in people being lost because of the claims of this false religion on the origin of the true Scriptures.

Of the belief systems only one (Christianity) is the absolute truth, and Satan knows it. So, he makes imitations that sound good to lead people astray. If one belief does not do it for someone, they try another. And contrary to what many believe, all roads do not lead or point to the God of the Bible. Only true Christianity with Jesus as the means to salvation is the true way. It may seem intolerant or harsh to an unbeliever, but it is true.

Satan has ways to reach those who are seeking what appears to be a spiritual way by subtle perversions of Christianity. In fact, many of these beliefs claim or appear to be Christian, but are not. These false truths are a gamble and can lead a person to be lost forever. Jehovah's Witness, Mormonism, Christian Science, Universalism, Islam, etc., are all examples. And one who reads this might say, "That's not true. How do you know that? I'm a Christian, or I do the best I can. I feel it is right." And I would say, "Why take the chance when you have the Old and New Testaments to show you the truth?"

The main difference between true Christianity and most other beliefs is performance to be saved. Christianity is the only belief that is based on God's love and his free gift of salvation. There is no performance or works to be saved. Christians do works because they are saved and love God, not to get saved. Christianity is a relationship with God. Once a person is a true believer and is filled with the Holy Spirit, they will discern better all other belief systems. They know salvation is by repenting of their sin and asking Jesus to be their Lord and Savior. They know that Jesus was the true Messiah prophesied in the Old Testament hundreds of years prior to his coming. They know that he was killed and He rose from the dead with many witnesses who saw and spoke to him. Above all, they know that Jesus is God (John 1:1–14), which is not what a false belief would adhere to.

2. What does Colossians 2:6–10 say about what Christians should do?

_____

_____

_____

_____

But, Satan will not give up even though he has lost the victory. He may even think he still has a chance to displace God. Now, he attacks God by pursuing man vigorously. One man lost to disbelief, deception, or an imitation religion is one more that God will lose forever in hell. Satan will use his demons and fallen man to distort the truths of the Christian faith to achieve this. A person can be deceived in their belief and, even if they are sincere, they will lose their eternity with God if they don't have Jesus as Lord and Savior. That is why it is important that Christians, especially new ones are discipled by true believers. *No wonder for even Satan disguises himself as an angel of light, therefore it is not surprising if his servants also disguise themselves as servants of righteousness whose end will be according to their deeds.* (2 Corinthians 11:14–15, NASB).

3. What do the following Scriptures say about Satan?

Job 1:7

_____

_____

_____

1 Peter 5:8

4. What does Satan need in order to attack us, according to Luke 22:31–32?

One of the most dangerous things about false teaching is that sometimes even the well-intentioned can be blinded and deceived. It sounds good to people, and they like what is said. *For the time will come that they will not endure sound doctrine; but wanting their ears tickled they shall accumulate for themselves teachers in accordance to their own desires, and will turn away their ears from the truth and will turn aside to myths* (2 Timothy 4:3, NASB). *And Jesus answered and said to them, many will come in My name, saying I am the Christ, and will mislead many* (Matthew 24:4, NASB).

5. If we cannot depend on what others say as true, how can we know that something we hear is true, according to Acts 17:11–12?

Christians believe that Jesus is the Son of God, and He teaches that the Bible is the very Word of God. Based on His infallible authority, we can trust that the Bible is God's inerrant Word. So, if we know that all Scripture in the Bible is God-breathed (2 Timothy 3:16), we know it is true. If we know that it is true, we know that there is a personal God who loves us, and we can measure all we see and hear to His biblical standard. This is what we as Christians can do to help discern the truth.

Truth is Absolute

We also know that truth is absolute and not relative as the world sees it. The world believes that if a belief is true for you, and that is what you really believe, then it is your truth to live by. This "live and let live" attitude is false because truth is absolute and not relative. If by relative thinking I personally believe that putting my hand in a fire will not burn me, I will be burned anyway. It does not matter whether I believe it or not. Fire burns, and that is an absolute truth. This is the way the world is deceived about the truths about God. They believe false beliefs to be true. They say to themselves, I believe these facts to be true for me; therefore, such is my life and my eternity. Even though we have the truth before us in Scripture, the world cannot see it.

Those who are in the cults may only answer to their leaderships who add to and take Scripture out of context to control those that follow them. They claim to have a purer expression of the truth. Their truth is perverted just enough to sound good and keep people lost. When their followers question them or have not adhered to complete obedience, they are disciplined, threatened with damnation, or kicked out of the cult.

Cults will change what they believe to be the truth because truth is not absolute to them. They will change it to accommodate their belief for today. An example is one cult predicted that Jesus was coming on dates in the past. This was false prophecy. Jesus did not come on their dates. God spoke about false prophets in Deuteronomy 18:20. When I inquired of one of the cult members about this, he said they no longer claim to be prophets.

God's truths do not change (Malachi 3:6a). They are absolute. Cults change their doctrine according to the times and their needs; their truth is relative. They believe in false doctrine even though they are sincere. We must be discerning, loving, and patient with them as we tell them God's truth. They often profess to be Christians and call what they believe the truth. But through careful examination of God's Word, we see that they are apostate.

6. How does Jesus describe Himself in John 14:6?

_____

_____

_____

_____

There are also many other false beliefs of man. The following is a summary of some of these:

Atheism says that no God actually exists.
Agnosticism says that there is not enough knowledge to know God exists.
Materialism says that everything can be explained by reference to reality.
Polytheism says that there are many gods.
Pantheism says god is everything, and everything is god.

Pane theism says the universe is god's body.

Deism says there is a God, but He is not involved in the direction of His creation.

Positivism rejects the existence of God because knowledge is restricted only to circumstance and phenomena.

Dualism says that there always two opposing principles.

Monism says God is one divine essence.

Post Modernism says I am my own truth. There is a "no truth" basis for life.

With so many people being deceived, it is important for a Christian not only to know the truth, but also to learn to be a persuasive Christian. We should be contagious in our evangelism. We do this by studying and reading our Bibles. We should know why we believe what we do and why we make the moral choices we do. Above all, we should be caring Christians. Ask God to give you the heart of a caring person. We should love other people, especially non-Christians. We must be able to tell anyone why we believe and that what we believe is true.

False Beliefs about the Resurrection

Another example we should know is Satan's personal attack on Jesus. Since the crucifixion of Jesus, there have been many false beliefs concerning it. The main truth being attacked is His resurrection, which is the crowning proof of our Christian faith. Without it, Christianity would also be a false religion (1 Corinthians 15:12–20). But it did take place, so our Christianity is an absolute truth. It proves Christ is God!

7. What do the following Scriptures say about the resurrection?

1 Thessalonians 1:10

_____

_____

_____

_____

Romans 8:11

_____

_____

_____

_____

John 2:19–21

_____

_____

_____

_____

Attacks on the resurrection include that Jesus was given a drug and was not really dead, that the cool air of the tomb woke Him up after three days, and that He rolled the two-ton stone away in His weakened state to get out. But the soldiers saw that He was dead; one soldier stabbed Him with his spear. The ruling Roman leader, Pilot, also certified the death of Jesus (Mark 15:44).

Another claim was that the disciples, the soldiers, the Roman authorities, or the Jews stole His Body because there was no body to be found. This could not have happened because it would have meant death to those who would do such a thing, as well as to the soldiers guarding the sealed tomb. No Body was later produced to prove that Jesus was dead or a fraud. In place of producing the body to silence His followers, the Jews remained silent. The disciples found the grave clothes intact (John 20:5-7). The empty tomb to this day is unanswerable evidence. John 20:1–10 reveals the reality of the tomb being empty. He was raised like He said. Even His followers, at the time, did not understand His resurrection. *For as yet they did not understand the Scripture that He must rise again from the dead* (John 20:9, NASB).

His disciples did not at first understand the resurrection prophecies about the Messiah. They did not expect to see Him after His crucifixion. They later did and preached it. They were later willing to die for their faith! Their lives were changed by the resurrection as they saw, touched, heard, and ate with Jesus afterward. Many saw Him for days after the resurrection, so must we be convinced and able to tell others about Jesus boldly.

Chapter 11

Spiritual Warfare

Today we see the sacredness of marriages broken down and a continuing slide of morals and values in our world. Escalation of crime seems to be everywhere. People appear as if they do not know the difference between right and wrong. *2 Timothy 3:1–5 says, "But realize this, in the last days difficult times will come. For men will be lovers of self, lovers of money, boastful, arrogant, revilers, disobedient to parents, ungrateful, unholy, unloving, irreconcilable, malicious gossips, without self-control, brutal, haters of good, treacherous, reckless, conceited, lovers of pleasure rather than lovers of God, holding to a form of godliness, although they have denied its power; Avoid such men as these"* (NASB).

The world does not know the strength of the enemy (Satan) who is behind most problems. In most cases, the world does not care or even believe in Satan. To the world, belief of Satan is primitive or a superstition. In this age of amazing technology, the devil is not real. To belief in him and his demons is regarded as foolish; to the world, a person borders on being a lunatic if he or she does. Disbelief in evil spiritual principalities, and even God, is put into the minds of people by Satan and his followers. Satan has blinded the minds of entire societies.

1. According to the following Scriptures, what are two objectives Satan has in 2 Corinthians 4:4 and 1 Thessalonians 2:18?

_____

_____

_____

_____

When a person becomes a Christian they begin to see the truth by the help of the Holy Spirit and Scripture. We see that human ways of going against evil are not going to work; the Bible says so. A spiritual battle is fought with spiritual weapons. It is a cosmic battle between God and His truth versus the devil and his deceptions; all created beings are involved. The cost has eternal ramifications. The casualties are the souls of people.

This is a battle that is fought by the redeemed. Unbelievers are not part of this because they do not see it, even though the enemy uses and manipulates them. They are in rebellion against God. We are to resist Satan until he is finally done away with. Until then the conflict between evil and good will continue. Through it, God will build His Church and grow His kingdom. Jesus won the battle at the cross for those who are saved and ultimately, God will be glorified by His creation.

Genesis 3:15 is a prophecy from God to Satan at the time of man's fall: *And I will put enmity between you and the women and between your seed and her seed. He shall bruise you on the head, and you shall bruise Him on the heel* (NASB). 1 John 3:8 tells us Jesus came to defeat the devil: *The one who practices sin is of the devil; for the devil has sinned from the beginning. The Son of God appeared for this purpose, to destroy the works of the devil* (NASB). In John 12:31–33, Jesus spoke of going to the cross: *Now judgment is upon this world; now the ruler of this world will be cast out. And I, if I am lifted up from the earth, will draw all men to myself. But He was saying this to indicate the kind of death by which He was to die* (NASB).

Satan pursues God's Church to persecute it, simply because it is composed of God's people. For this reason, Paul says we need to put on the full armor of God (Ephesians 6:10–18), know God's Word, and pray. From our standpoint of victory in Christ, Christians fight the battle. We do not fight for victory that has been done. We fight the enemy, knowing he has been defeated.

Even though Satan has lost at the cross, he attacks us with the intention to make us stumble and sin. He wants to cripple our faith and disrupt our spiritual lives. Satan wants us to forget God's blessings and promises for His people. He wants to cast doubts in us. He wants to deceive us and get us to live our lives without Jesus. He wants us to be caught up in heresy and false doctrine instead of Christian truths. He will provide opportunities for you to sin, will make sin look good, will desensitize you to it, and make its seriousness appear lessened. He will tell you to go ahead and sin, since it is easy to repent later. He will tell you the lie that you are missing a lot by living a holy life. The devil wants to get back at God and prevent the Lord from receiving the glory He is worthy of. Remember, the victory is God's. Colossians 2:14–15 says, *"Having cancelled out the certificate of debt consisting of decrees against us, which was hostile to us; and He has taken it out of the way, having nailed it to the cross. When He had disarmed the rulers and authorities, He made a public display of them, having triumphed over them through Him*" (NASB).

2. According to the following Scriptures, what has God done to show that He is victorious over Satan?

John 16:11

_____

_____

_____

_____

John 12:31

_____

_____

_____

_____

2 Corinthians 4:3–6

_____

_____

_____

_____

Mark 3:27

_____

_____

_____

_____

Colossians 2:15

_____

_____

_____

Hebrews 2:14–15

3. What does John 17:15 say Jesus prayed for concerning His followers?

_____

_____

_____

_____

4. What can the devil do to a true believer, according to 1 John 5:18?

_____

_____

_____

_____

5. In 1 John 4:1–4, how do we recognize the Spirit of Truth?

_____

_____

_____

_____

We must stay alert and continue to watch and pray. We need to remember that it is a battle that is fought in the heavenly realm. The enemy knows where our weaknesses are, so we put on the armor of God. When Satan attacks, it could be a surprise as we see in the first chapter of Job. He may be disguised as a person or an angel, or he may be invisible (his spirit form). He could question God's Word, as he did with Eve and Jesus. The enemy may begin his attacks by placing thoughts in a person's mind and trying to affect emotions. This is where the battle begins and where it should be dealt with.

Satan will use temptation as his primary strategy. He can encourage the thoughts of temptation within us. He tries to persuade us that temptation satisfied is better than God's way. If he succeeds, he has put a rift between you and God. Whether it is a moral or a purity issue, fellowship with God is hindered. The enemy can now move on to condemning you, causing anxiety, and feelings of guilt. He wants to hinder or stop your walk with God and your service.

Scripture says that God has promised a way to escape temptation. There is always an escape. 1 Cor. 10:13 says, *"No temptation has overtaken you but such as is common to man; and God is faithful, who will not allow you to be tempted beyond what you are able, but with the temptation will provide the way of escape also, so that you will be able to endure it* (NASB).

6. What does 1Peter 5:8–9 say about believers and the adversary?

_____

_____

_____

_____

The enemy likes to attack believers after a spiritual high moment or something good God has done in your life. Satan does not change his tactics much. He still uses what has worked well for him throughout history. The Bible says he uses the lust or desire of the flesh, the lust or desire of the eyes, and the pride of life as the ways he attacks man. A good example of temptation is Satan's temptation of Jesus, as recorded in Matthew 4:3–11.

Satan uses temptation on the Lord after a significant spiritual event—His baptism and the Father saying He is pleased with Him. Jesus goes into the wilderness to be tested as He fasted for forty days. Satan comes to Him three times with three different temptations. Jesus uses Scripture as His way of escape and does not fall prey to the devil's tactics.

7. Read Matthew 4:1–11. What does Jesus do when Satan tempts Him?

_____

_____

_____

_____

Another way Satan attacks us is through accusations. Revelation 12:10 says, *"Then I heard a loud voice in heaven saying, now the salvation, and the power, and the kingdom of our God and the authority of His Christ have come, and the accuser of our brethren has been thrown down, he who accuses them before our God day and night* (NASB).

Satan will attempt to cause disunity between believers. We are God's Church, and we should show the Glory of God to each other and a depraved world. What better way is there than for Satan to attack the Lord this way? Satan will also accuse us in our minds by showing us our sin and weaknesses. He does this to give us feelings of condemnation and hopelessness. But, we have the Holy Spirit in us to show us our sin and the way out from it by His love, grace, mercy, and forgiveness. He has also equipped His followers for the battle so they can live as Christians and minister in this world by God's will.

The Armor of God

Ephesians 6:10–18 says, *"Finally, be strong in the Lord and in the strength of His might. Put on the full armor of God, so that you will be able to stand firm against the schemes of the devil. For our struggle is not against flesh and blood, but against the rulers, against the powers, against the world forces of this darkness, against the spiritual forces of wickedness in the heavenly places. Therefore take up the full armor of God, so that you will be able to resist in the evil day, and having done everything, to stand firm. Stand firm therefore, having girded your loins with truth, and having put on the breastplate of righteousness, and having shod your feet with the preparation of the gospel of peace, in addition to all, taking up the shield of faith with which you will be able to extinguish all the flaming arrows of the evil one. And take up the helmet of salvation and the sword of the spirit which is the Word of God. With all prayer and petition pray at all times in the spirit, and with this in view be on the alert with all perseverance and petition for all saints* (NASB).

Part of being prepared for spiritual warfare is to know what weapons you have at your disposal as a Christian. You will be confronted with spiritual opposition even if you do not want it. Are you familiar with your strengths and weaknesses? Do you understand how serious the adversary is about bringing you down? You must be familiar with Satan's tactics and how he wages war. We must know what armor God has provided for us, and how to use it.

First, Paul tells us in Ephesians 6:10 to be strong in the Lord and the strength of His might. It starts with recognizing that it is not all you and it is not all God. It is both God and you; you act in God's power and strength through faith.

8. What does Philippians 4:13 say we can do and how can we do it?

_____

_____

_____

_____

You are not strong in the Lord by your own effort. It is by recognizing our weaknesses and remembering what God has done to prepare you. It is by His Word. We are strong when we are obedient and abiding in Him (John 15). We are strong when we continually build ourselves up in faith (Jude 20). We become stronger when we realize the reasons for our trials. We are stronger when we see that His grace is sufficient for our weaknesses. *And He said to me, "My grace is sufficient for you, for power is perfected in weakness." Most gladly therefore, I will rather boast about my weaknesses, so that the power of Christ may dwell in me* (2 Corinthians 12:9, NASB).

9. What does James 4:7–8 say we must do?

_____

_____

_____

_____

In Ephesians 6:11 we are told to put on *God's armor*, every piece, and not to leave any part off. Every true believer is expected to do this because it is not done for us. Satan will know if you have left a piece of armor behind. We put on the armor so that we will be able to stand firm and not be moved by the adversary when he attacks, which is referred to the evil day.

The Roman soldier's armor is a good example of what we as Christians should put on. The armor is basically six pieces. The first three are put on and continually worn for readiness. The second three are put on when the attacks come. When they come, the Roman soldier grabs his helmet, shield, sword, and goes to battle. All pieces are put on in order, and so it is with our armor of God.

Gird Your Loins with Truth, Ephesians 6:14

The first piece of armor a soldier would put on is a belt to gird his waist. The undergarment or tunic that he wore would need to be tied securely to this belt so no loose parts would hinder his movement. This belt was worn at all times to keep the soldier ready for attack. We are also to be ready at all times with the belt of truth. *Luke 12:35 says, "Be dressed ready for service and keep your lamps burning"* (NIV). 1 Peter 1:13 says, *"Therefore, prepare your minds for action, keep sober in spirit, fix your hope completely on his grace to be brought to you at the revelation of Jesus Christ"* (NASB).

We are to put on the truth provided by God inwardly and outwardly. When we do this, we can defend ourselves against the false teachings and the deceptions from the devil. We will stand firm in the truth we have from God. This will also affect our desire to have integrity and be honest within ourselves. When we are saved and have the truth of God, we are filled with the Holy Spirit and His Word in us. We need to believe and be confident that we have and know His truth in us. So we must read, study, and memorize His Word. When attacks come, we declare the Scriptures we know, believe, and that are brought to mind by the Holy Spirit.

10. According to Acts 20:27–31, what was Paul's fear of what would happen after he departed?

_____

_____

_____

11. John 14:6 says we are to put on what?

_____

_____

_____

_____

The Breastplate of Righteousness, Ephesians 6:14

The breastplate was the second piece of armor put on by the Roman soldier after the belt was used to gird his loins. The breastplate would attach to the belt and cover the torso to the neck. It would protect the soldier from direct hits from a sword or arrow.

The breastplate of righteousness is Christ's righteousness imputed on believers through the gospel; it is a free gift to us from God by grace and faith. It is not by our works, but by Christ's only. When we have on the righteousness of God, we are able to defend ourselves against the attacks from the devil. We will be able to stand against his accusations concerning our sin and failures.

Romans 1:16-17 says, "For I am not ashamed of the gospel, for it is the power of God for salvation to everyone who believes, to the Jew first, and also to the Greek. For in it the righteousness of God is revealed from faith to faith; as it is written, but the righteous man shall live by faith" (NASB). _Philippians 3:9 says, "And may be found in Him, not having a righteousness of my own derived from the law, but that which is through faith in Christ, the righteousness which comes from God on the basis of faith"_ (NASB).

12. What is Jesus Christ our Lord called in Jeremiah 23:6?

_____

_____

_____

_____

The breastplate of righteousness does not mean that we look to our personal righteousness. In times of attack, it is being confident that you know the truth and proclaim it. It is recognizing that you have been imputed with Christ's righteousness. We must be in the Word, know the Word, pray always, and put on the Lord Jesus Christ.

Shoes of the Gospel of Peace, Ephesians 6:15

The shoes of the gospel of peace are the third piece of armor a Christian should put on to stand firm and engage the enemy. The shoes gave the Roman soldier confidence in his stance, not having to worry about slipping in battle. A Christian is to be sure they know and believe the gospel of peace, which is the gospel of Christ. 1 Corinthians 15:1–4 says, *"Now I make known to you, brethren, the gospel which I preached to you, which also you received, in which also you stand, by which also you are saved, if you hold fast the word which I preached to you, unless you believed in vain. For I delivered to you as of first importance what I also received, that Christ died for our sins according to the Scriptures, and that He was raised on the third day according to the Scriptures"* (NASB).

Satan tries to undermine our footing by casting doubts and fears, but we have sure footing when we know we stand firm with the gospel of peace. When we do, Satan will not spoil our peace and wellbeing.

13. What does Romans 5:1–2 say we have as believers?

_____

_____

_____

_____

Stand firm when you are attacked because you remember who you are. You are a child of God, washed by His Blood. You have a testimony, eternal life with God, and Christ's righteousness, and you are forgiven. Believe and have confidence that these things are true for you as a Christian. John 14:27 says, *"Peace I leave with you; My peace I give to you; not as the world gives do I give to you. Do not let your heart be troubled, nor let it be fearful"* (NASB). Colossians 3:15 says, *"Let the peace of Christ rule in your hearts, to which indeed you were called in one body; and be thankful"* (NASB).

14. What does Isaiah 26:3 say about how we are kept in *perfect* peace?

_____

_____

_____

_____

The Shield of Faith, Ephesians 6:16

The shield of faith is the fourth piece of armor the Christian is to put on. The Roman soldier had a shield that was about four feet long. The shield would protect most of his body, and he could easily crouch behind it. The shield was covered with a material that would be dampened so that the flaming arrows of the enemy would go out.

Spiritually we are attacked in our minds. That is where Satan starts his battles. He puts thoughts in our minds, accuses us, tries to cast doubt, and tries to put feelings in our minds. Satan wants to depress you and make you feel that you are less than you are in the Lord. With the shield of faith, we put out the fiery darts (Satan-produced thoughts) in our minds. God has provided a way so that they do not hit their target. He has provided a way so that we can defend ourselves against the attacks that will come.

When we are attacked, it is against our faith in God's truth. It is then that we exercise our faith in God's truth to overcome the thoughts, lies, and doubts Satan puts in our minds. When we do this, we are applying the belt of truth (the truth of God), the breastplate of righteousness (our imputed righteousness from God), and the gospel of God (Shoes with the preparation of the gospel of peace). We are applying the first Four pieces of armor.

15. Read Proverbs 30:5. What does it say?

_____

_____

_____

_____

The Helmet of Salvation, Ephesians 6:17

This is the fifth piece of armor the Christian must put on. The Roman helmet was to prevent death blows to the head. When a Christian puts on the helmet of salvation understanding his or her salvation and knowing it to be true is important. You should set your sight on things above. First, when you are being attacked, knowing what God has done in your salvation concerning the past is that He has justified you. You are declared righteous and have all your sins forgiven. You must be assured that God has done this for you.

Second, you must know what God has done in the present concerning your salvation, which is that He is now sanctifying you. Know and be sure that you are being delivered from your sin in the present. The third and final thing you need to know about your salvation is in the future. God promises to glorify you in Him. He will totally deliver you from any and all presence of sin forever, and by this God is glorified. *1 Thessalonians 5:8–10* says to put on the hope of your salvation: "*But since we are of the day, let us be sober having put on the breastplate of faith and love, and as a helmet, the hope of our salvation. For God has not destined us for wrath, but for obtaining salvation through our Lord Jesus Christ, who died for us, so that whether we are awake or asleep, we will live together with Him*" (NASB).

16. How does Colossians 3:1–3 help us to put on the hope of our salvation?

_____

_____

_____

_____

The Sword of the Spirit, Ephesians 6:17

The sword is the sixth piece of armor a Christian is to put on and use in defense for resisting the enemy. The Roman soldier would defend himself with a short two-edged sword in close hand-to-hand combat. The soldier's sword was his only way of fighting back and causing harm to the enemy. The enemy, realizing this, would flee and be driven back. When a Christian is attacked, he or she is to take up the sword that belongs to the Spirit, given to Christians to be used by the Spirit's power. We must have God's Word (Scripture) in our hearts. The Holy Spirit brings it to remembrance for us to use. We speak it, and the Spirit makes it effective. This is how the enemy is defended against and caused to flee. When we do this, it is done with faith and the knowledge that, by the Spirit's power, the enemy will be driven back.

17. According to James 4:6–8, how are you to be, and what will God do for you if you are?

_____

_____

_____

_____

1 Peter 5:8–9 says, *"Be of sober spirit, be on alert. Your adversary, the devil, prowls around like a roaring lion seeking someone to devour. But resist him firm in your faith knowing that the same experiences of suffering are being accomplished by your brethren who are in the world"* (NASB). A Christian will have opposition from Satan with every step in the Lord he takes towards growth and service for God. This is a spiritual battle that must be fought by putting on the armor of God and recognizing how the enemy attacks us.

Chapter 12

Sharing Your Faith

Giving the saving message of the gospel to a lost world is of utmost importance to God. We may be Christians now, but once we were not. We were part of the world we are trying to reach. God used someone to reach us and give us the gospel; thus, God wants us to do the same with our lives, with our testimonies and words, telling people how they may be saved. When you were saved, Jesus was also saying to you what He said to His disciples, "Follow Me and I will make you fishers of men." He not only saves us from eternal hell, but asks us to work with Him to save others as well. Christ asks us to make disciples of others as Christians. We don't share the gospel alone. The Holy Spirit is with us when we do. 2 Corinthians 5:18–21 says, *"Now all these things are from God, who reconciled us to Himself through Christ and gave us the ministry of reconciliation, namely that God was in Christ reconciling the world to Himself, not counting their trespasses against them, and He has committed to us the word of reconciliation"* (NASB).

We are called to evangelize a hostile world that, for the most part, does not like believers. The world does not understand who God is or His ways; therefore, they cannot understand the Christian who is called to give them the message of the gospel. Nevertheless, the Lord has provided the gospel for everyone. Because of this hostile world, we will experience persecution. Another reason is that the world does not like hearing that they are sinners and fall short, morally, to God's standard. The world will not know where they stand with God unless their sin is exposed. Only God by His Spirit can help them hear and respond to the gospel. John 15:22-23 says, *"If I had not spoken to them, they would not have sin, but now they have no excuse for their sin. He who hates Me hates My Father also"* (NIV).

Whether you have been a Christian for a long time or have just become one, you can tell others about Jesus. Some people think they are not ready or do not know what to say. Others feel they need to know more about the Bible or feel scared to let people know that they are Christians. They might be afraid of being made fun of. Those are not reasons to shrink back from telling others about

Christ. All you really need is your testimony and some verses from Scripture that will relate truths. Most importantly, you must be filled with the Holy Spirit and living a life of obedience to God.

The truth is, God does the saving, and we are just to tell people the good news of the gospel. God may use you to pray with people to receive Christ. What a blessing to be used by God in that manner. We should seek a decision when we witness. But don't expect all to respond that way. When you help lead someone to Christ this way, your witness has been effectual. Remember, God is asking you to share with others by the power of the Holy Spirit in you and the gospel. This same Holy Spirit will give you the words to use when you ask Him. *Acts 1:8 says, "But you will receive power when the Holy Spirit has come upon you; and you shall be my witnesses both in Jerusalem, and in all Judea, and Samaria, and even to the remotest part of the earth"* (NASB). Luke 15:10 says, *"I tell you there is joy in the presence of the angels of God over one sinner who repents"* (NASB).

1. Why does Paul say he is not ashamed to proclaim the gospel in Romans 1:16?

_____

_____

_____

_____

2. What does Jesus say He will do for those who follow Him, according to Matthew 4:19?

_____

_____

3. What does Proverbs 11:30 say a wise person does?

_____

_____

When sharing the gospel, it is important that you use the truth of God's Word as much as possible; His Word is living and does not come back void. People may say they don't believe what it says, but it will still have an effect.

4. Read Hebrews 4:12 and write what it says about God's Word.

_____

_____

_____

_____

If you find it hard to speak to people about Jesus, ask the Lord in prayer to help you. Ask Him for strength and for the Holy Spirit to help you. Ask Him to help you see unbelievers as God does. Jesus saw people in a certain way in the following Scripture: *Seeing the people, He felt compassion for them, because they were distressed and dispirited like sheep without a shepherd. Then He said to His disciples, the harvest is plentiful, but the workers are few. Therefore beseech the Lord of the harvest to send out workers into His harvest* (Matthew 9:36–38, NASB).

5. The disciples were being persecuted for proclaiming the gospel. They did not pray to have the persecution stop, but they prayed for something else. What was it, in Acts 4:23–31?

_____

_____

_____

_____

Paul outlines what he shares when talking about the gospel in the Scriptures below:

For I delivered to you as of first importance what I also received, that Christ died for our sins according to the Scriptures, and that He was buried, and that He was raised on the third day according to the Scriptures (1 Corinthians 15:3–4, NASB).

Conduct yourselves with wisdom toward outsiders, making the most of the opportunity. Let your speech always be with grace as though seasoned with salt, so that you will know how you should respond to each person (Colossians 4:5–6, NASB).

6. What are we to do and why, according to 2 Timothy 2:24–26 and 1 Peter 3:15?

_____

_____

_____

_____

When talking to someone about Jesus, you should make the gospel of utmost importance, but there are also other things about Jesus that are helpful for people to know: That Jesus is not only the Son of God, but that He is the second person of the Godhead. Jesus created all things and has always existed (John: 1–14, Colossians 2:9). They should know that there is no other name by which a person can be saved and have eternal life (Acts 4:12).

7. The following verses will help you when you are telling people about the free gift of salvation and that they need Jesus as Savior and Lord of their lives. Look them up in your Bible and write them as they are.

All unsaved people are in the same lost condition (Romans 3:23).

_____

_____

_____

_____

There is a price to pay for sin (Romans 6:23).

_____

_____

_____

_____

God paid the price (Romans 5:8).

_____

_____

_____

_____

Jesus is Lord and God raised Him from death (Romans 10:9).

_____

_____

_____

Those that believe and receive Him are saved (John 1:12).

_____

_____

_____

He died for our sins (1 Peter 2:24).

_____

_____

_____

_____

Man cannot save himself (Mark 10:26–27).

_____

_____

8. How can you be an ambassador in your life? Who can you reach for Christ?

_____

_____

_____

_____

Matthew 5:14–16 says, *"You are the light of the world. A city set on a hill cannot be hidden; nor does anyone light a lamp and put it under a basket, but on the lamp stand, and it gives light to all that are in the house, Let your light shine before men in such a way that they may see your good works, and glorify your Father who is in heaven"* (NASB).

Chapter 13

Living for His Coming

One of the amazing things about Scripture is that we know how it's all going to end. For us as believers, it is a beginning of an indescribable eternity with God: We will be with our Lord and have glorified bodies; many of life's mysteries will be unfolded; and we will be in a perfect kingdom with no sin, death, or pain. God will be glorified by His creation. We will love and worship Him forever, for He is worthy.

But what do we do in the mean time? Do we just wait for His coming? No we don't. We do what His Word says: We love others, serve Him, and serve others. We get involved in our churches and ministries. We share the gospel and live as examples. We live obedient lives according to His Word.

Living by the Spirit

But I say, walk by the spirit, and you will not carry out the desires of the flesh (Galatians 5:16, NASB).

The Bible says that if we live by the Spirit we will not carry out the desires of the flesh. We are all at a certain place of growth with God concerning this verse, yet we are called to live our Christian life this way. The Scripture says that any living we do apart from God will result in our carrying out fleshly desires. Our flesh is still fallen and seeks its own way; therefore, we need the Holy Spirit in us to guide us. You may feel the flesh wanting to overpower you, but don't give in. If you are a Christian the Holy Spirit is inside and with you.

1. What does Gal. 5:10–21 say the deeds of the flesh are?

_____

_____

_____

_____

Eph. 5:3–13?

_____

_____

_____

_____

2. If a person practices these deeds of the flesh, what does Gal. 5:21 say about them?

_____

_____

_____

When we slip and sin, Scripture says we are to confess it to God and ask for forgiveness, and He will forgive us. When we walk by the Spirit, we live by the Fruit of the Spirit. Galatians 5:22–23 says, *"But the fruit of the spirit is love, joy, peace, patience, kindness, goodness, faithfulness, gentleness, self-control."*

So, we walk by the Spirit by realizing how the power of the flesh can affect us. We also know we have the Holy Spirit in us, so we can deny the desires of the flesh. Know that the flesh is nailed to the cross and that Christ is Lord of your life. Say no to the flesh and give it to God; crucify the flesh and leave it on the cross. Mark 8:34-35 says, *"And He summoned the multitude with the disciples and said to them, "If anyone wishes to come after Me, let him deny himself, and take up his cross and follow Me. For whoever wishes to save his life shall lose it; but whoever loses his life for My sake and the gospel shall save it"* (NASB).

Walking in the Spirit is being in His Word and in daily prayer. In the Spirit, we worship and have fellowship with other believers. We regularly confess our sins and obey His Word. Walking in the Spirit means trusting God, taking part in the Lord's table, and serving. It is giving of our time, talents, and treasures for the kingdom of God. We do it all with the fruits of the Spirit and love for God.

Just as we are not to walk in the flesh, we are also not to walk in this world as the world does. Christians are just passing through; this is not our home. We are eternal, and this world is temporal. Believers are called to love God and live in the Spirit in a world that hates God. We are sent into the world as lights and examples to those who are perishing. Before Jesus went to the cross, He prayed the following on behalf of all believers: *I have given them Thy word; and the world has hated them, because they are not of the world, even as I am not of the world. I do not ask thee to take them out of the world, but to keep them from the evil one. They are not of the world, even as I am not of the world. Sanctify them in the truth. Thy word is truth. As thou didst send Me into the world, I also have sent them into the world* (John 17:14–18, NASB).

Our strength and power does not come from this world; our life and strength are from God. We are born from above. Because we are set apart from this world, what better reason is there to make a life that counts for eternity?

Ready for His Coming

Although we do not know when the Lord will come, we can see the signs described in Scripture already happening (Matthew 24). Scripture says He can come at any time. Revelation 22:7 says, *"And behold, "I am coming quickly, blessed is he who heeds the prophecy of this book"* (NASB). 1 Corinthians 15:23 says, *"But each in his own order, Christ the first fruits, after that those who are in Christ at His coming"* (NASB).

Jesus said that when Christians see the signs, it is the beginning of birth pangs culminating in His coming to set up His kingdom. The signs tell us that the seven-year tribulation we read of in the books of Revelation and Daniel is coming soon This will be a time of suffering for the whole world. When Christians see these signs, we are to look up because He can take us at any moment. There are many beliefs within the church that give different times for the rapture—our meeting Him in the air and going to heaven with Him. If you are ready, then for you, it does not matter when He comes. You know you will be with Him when He does. Are you ready? He will come for His church very soon. This could be the next event in history.

Because you have obeyed my command to persevere, I will protect you from the great time of testing that will come upon the whole world to test those who belong to this world (Rev. 3:10, NLT).

Behold I tell you a mystery; we shall not all sleep, but we shall all be changed, in a moment, in a twinkling of an eye, at the last trumpet; for the trumpet will sound and the dead will be raised imperishable and we shall be changed (1 Corinthians 15: 51–52, NASB).

Beloved now we are children of God and it not appeared as yet what we shall be. We know that when He appears we shall be like Him, because we shall see Him just as He is (1 John 3:2, NASB).

3. Read the parable of the ten virgins in Matthew 25:1–13. The virgins were preparing for the grooms arrival. Which of the two groups of virgins would you place yourself in right now?

_____

_____

_____

_____

What, if anything, do you believe you should do to be one of the wise virgins?

_____

_____

_____

_____

At the end of the tribulation, Jesus will come back in glory to destroy the enemies of God: the nations will be judged; Satan will be bound; and the Lord will set up His kingdom on earth for one thousand years. After the one thousand years, all the wicked dead (who are not in the Lamb's Book of Life) will stand before Christ and be judged at the white thrown judgment. The wicked will not escape their destiny, but all good and bad will declare Christ as Lord. The wicked dead, Satan, and his followers will be cast into the lake of fire forever. From Scripture, this appears to be an eternal conscious abode of torment. Christians will be with God in heaven where there will no longer be sin, pain, suffering, and death; we will worship and praise God forever.

Be Ready for His Coming

Appendix—Answers to Study Questions

Chapter 2—Answers on the True Believer's Assurance

1. Romans 6:1–16, v. 6, My old self was crucified with Christ, and I am no longer a slave to sin. V. 11, Consider myself dead to sin. Consider myself alive in Christ Jesus. V. 13, Yield to God and do not yield to sin. V. 16, whom you would yield yourself to.
2. Romans 5:1–2, We have been made right in the sight of God by our faith.

3. 1 John 5:11–12, The Word says believers have eternal life if they have the Son.

4. I Cor. 6:11, Because of what God did for us, we are made right in Him.

5. Galatians 4:6, Romans 8:16, The Holy Spirit is lives in us and tells our spirits.

6. Romans 8:1, There is no condemnation for those who have received Christ.

7. 1 John 5:13, We know that we have eternal life because we believe in the name of the Son of God.

8. 2 Corinthians 6:17, a new creation.

9. Romans 3:12–19, No one does that which is good. They lie and curse. They are destructive and violent. They have no peace and are miserable. They do not fear God.

10. John 6:37, All the people that the Father draws and gives to Jesus will come to Jesus for salvation, and Jesus will not reject them.

11. John 6:38–39, Jesus did not come to do His own will, but the Father's will. The Father's will is that Jesus will not lose anyone who comes to Him, and He will resurrect them to eternal life.

12. Romans 8:29–39, Write in your own words. Death, life, angels, principalities, powers, things present, things to come, height, depth, any other creature. There is nothing in your life that separates you from the love of God.

13. John 16:1–8, We must remain (abide) in Him by relationship and obedience to His commands. Then we will bear fruit. If we do not bear fruit, we are not remaining in Jesus. Those that do not bear fruit are lifeless and probably not true believers. Apart from obeying Jesus and following His commands, we cannot bear fruit. When we obey, we bear fruit. God answers our prayers. All these things give us assurance that we are born again.

14. James 1:22, Do what the Word says, instead of just listening to it, so you won't be deceived into thinking you're okay with God.

Chapter 3—Answers on the Bible

1. 2 Peter 1:21 says that prophesy and Scripture are inspired by the Holy Spirit.
2. Matthew 5:17–18, He came to fulfill all the law and the prophets.
John 5:39, He said the Scriptures testify of Him that He is the way to eternal life.

3. 2 Peter 1:21, Acts 1:16, the Holy Spirit.

4. Luke 24:25–27, From Moses to the Prophets Jesus explained to them what was written of Him. If they did not believe the OT prophecies about Jesus, they were foolish. Luke 24:44-48, Jesus said that all things concerning Him were in the Scriptures.

5. Jesus fulfilled all that was written of Him in the Old Testament.

6. Jesus quoted Scripture in these attacks. He started with "It is written."

7. All temptation is common to man. He will not let us be tempted beyond what we can handle. He provides a way out.

Chapter 4—Answers on God, Jesus Christ, and the Holy Spirit

1. Philippians 2:7–8, Rewrite it in your own words.

2. John 10:30, He declares himself to be God.

3. John 1:3, He created all things. Colossians 1:15, He upholds the universe. John 2:19, He raised himself from the dead.

4. Matthew 28:20, His omnipresence. He is everywhere with His followers. Revelation 1:18, His omnipotence. His power is limitless. John 21:17, His omniscience. He has unlimited knowledge. John 17:5, He pre-existed. Christ did not have a beginning.

5. Isaiah 7:14, His coming was predicted hundreds of years earlier. Hebrews 10:7, His coming was part of God's eternal purpose.

6. John 14:9, He came to reveal the Father. 1 John 3:8, He came to destroy the works of the devil. Hebrews 9:26, He came to sacrifice Himself to put away sin. 1 Corinthians 15:3, His death was a substitute for all Christians.

7. Psalm 72, List some of the aspects of Jesus' reign.

8. Isaiah 40: 13–14, He is all-knowing or omniscient. Psalm 139:7, He is everywhere or omnipresent. Hebrews 9:14, He has no beginning or end. He is eternal.

9. 1 Corinthians 12:7–11, He gives believers manifestations of the Spirit. To each a particular one like wisdom, the word of knowledge, faith, healing, miracles, prophecy, distinguishing of spirits, tongues, and interpretation of tongues.

10. Acts 13:2, He told them to set apart certain ones for the work of the ministry while they were fasting and praying.

11. 1 Corinthians 3:16, The Holy Spirit dwells in us. John 14:15–16, The Holy Spirit dwells with us. John 7: 38–39, The Holy Spirit can overflow us (the baptism of the Spirit). At this point we are fully controlled by the Spirit. John 3:5, The Holy Spirit gives us spiritual life.
1Corinthians 12:13, you are then baptized into the body of Christ. Ephesians 4:30, The Holy Spirit seals you. Romans 8:16, The Holy Spirit bears witness with our spirits that we are God's children. Romans 8:26–27, The Holy Spirit intercedes for us in God's will and helps us with our prayers.

12. 1 Corinthians 6:19, Your body is the temple of the Holy Spirit.

13. Self-examination question for you to answer.

14. Romans 8:27, He searches hearts and intercedes for us according to God's will. John 16:15, The Holy Spirit bears witness of Christ.

15. 1 Corinthians 2:10–13, He searches all things from man to God because He is God. He knows the thoughts of God and man.

16. Luke 9:26, by being ashamed of Jesus Christ. Prov. 16:18, pride. Psalm 66:18, keeping wickedness and un-confessed sin in my heart. 1 John 2:15-17, worldly desires.

17. Self-examination question for you to answer.

18. When we pray according to His will, God answers our prayers. Hebrews 11:6 says that we must have faith to know He rewards those that do.

19. Trust in the Spirit to guide you. We have to be obedient to His Word. We have to avoid sin and get sin out of our lives. To confess any sins we have committed. To pray, worship and be in the Word. We need to deny ourselves and let the Spirit have His way.

Chapter 5—Answers on Angels and Man

1. Luke 20:34–36, They will be resurrected. They will not marry in heaven. They will not die anymore. They will be sons of God—like the angels in many ways, but not angels.
2. 1 Corinthians 6:2–3, we will judge the world and angels.

3. Write in your words what it means to you to be made in God's image.

Chapter 6—Answers on the Church

1. Revelation 21:3–4, God will dwell with His church, and its members will be His people. He will wipe away all tears, and there will no longer be death. There will be no mourning, crying, or pain. All these things will have passed away.
2. Acts 20:28, Jesus purchased the church with His own blood.

3. 1 Corinthians 16:19, Acts 20:7, They met in homes on Sundays.

4. Acts 2:42, They were continuing in the teaching of the apostles, fellowship, the breaking of bread, and prayer.

5. 1 Timothy 4:6–8, 11–13, As a leader he should be about the business of the church. Constantly be nourished on the words of the faith and sound doctrine. Pursue godliness because it profits now and in eternity. Prescribe and teach godliness. Be an example to others with the reading of Scripture, exhortation, and teaching.

6. Matthew 5:13–16, We are the salt of the earth, and we are not to lose our savor. We are lights and are not to hide our light. We must let our faith be known and proclaim it! By this we glorify God.

7. Ephesians 3:10, Through God's church, His wisdom will be known. 2 Corinthians 5:18–20, God is reaching others through the Church. We are ambassadors for Christ. Acts 1:8, The Church shall receive power and be a witness. 1 Peter 2:9, We are a chosen race so we can proclaim what God did to save us.

8. **Ephesus**, Revelation 2:7, I will grant to eat of the tree of life in God's paradise. **Smyrna**, Revelation 2:11, they shall not be hurt by the second death. **Pergamum**, Revelation 2:17, I will give them hidden manna; I will give them a white stone and new name. **Thyatira**, Revelation 2:2–29, I will give them authority to overcome nations and rule them with a rod of iron. God will give them the morning star. **Sardis**, Revelation 3:5–6, They will be clothed in a white garment, and their name will not be erased from the Book of Life. Jesus will confess their names before God and the angels. **Philadelphia**, Revelation 3:12–13, Jesus will make them a pillar in the temple of God. They will have on them the name of God and the name of His city, the New Jerusalem, and Jesus' new name.
Laodicea, Revelation 3:21–22, He will grant them to sit down with Jesus on His throne as He overcame and sits with His father on His throne.

Chapter 7—Answers on Our Obedience

1. 1John 2:3–4, We know Him if we obey Him. If we do not obey Him, we do not Know Him.
2. Matthew 7:21, Only those who do the will of the Father will be in heaven for eternity with God.

3. Romans 5:1–5, Suffering produces perseverance (endurance), character, and hope.

4. James 1:5–6, Ask for spiritual wisdom. Do it humbly and with faith.

5. James 1:12, They will receive the crown of life.

6. James 1:14–16, Temptation comes from our own evil desires. Where it is conceived it leads to sin, when we sin we start the dying process. Sin comes from inside our own hearts.

7. Ephesians 4:17, Don't walk in the ways of the world and practice sin like the world does. Christ has freed you from that.

8. Ephesians 4:25–5:21, Speak the truth; put off falsehood; do not sin when you are angry; do not stay angry, for it gives the devil a foothold; do not steal; be useful and work; share with those in need;

use no unwholesome speech; build others up; do not grieve the Holy Spirit; get rid of bitterness, rage anger, brawling, slander, and malice; be kind, forgiving and compassionate; allow no sexual immorality, no impurity, and no greed; be loving and imitate God; be thankful; allow no foolish talk; do not be deceived; be fruitful; avoid the fruitlessness of the dark; stop secret sin; be wise; know God's will for you; be filled with the Spirit; thank God in Christ; and submit to one another.

9. 1 Thessalonians 5: 21–22, Examine everything carefully and hold fast to what is good.

10. Philippians 4:8–9, Think on what is pure, lovely, admirable, and excellent, and worthy of praise and what is true, right, and noble. Follow Paul's example, and do what he taught. The Lord will be with you.

11. Romans 8:7, being controlled by the sinful nature, not submitting to God's law, and being hostile towards God.

12. Galatians 5:16, by living in the Spirit.

13. Some of these things might include: certain types of music, old crowds you use to hang with, old habits, certain types of movies, etc.

14. John 15:10, We will remain in His love. John 15:14, We are His friends. 1 John 3:22, God gives us anything we ask.

15. Self-examination question.

16. The spiritual truth here is that through baptism we died, are buried, and are raised to new life with Him.

17. Romans 10:17, Faith comes by hearing the Word of God.

18. Acts 20:21, Jesus Christ.

19. Living for Him and being obedient.

Chapter 8—Answers on Spiritual Gifts

1. Use them to serve others with grace. Do it all in Jesus Christ so God will be glorified.
2. If it is prophecy, let him do it according to his faith, if it is serving let him serve, if it is teaching let him teach, if it is contributing let him give generously, if it is mercy, let him do it cheerfully.

3. Without love it is nothing.

4. Love is patient, kind, does not envy, does not boast, is not proud, is not rude, is not self-seeking, and is not angered.

5. 2 Corinthians 5:7, faith
  James 1:5, wisdom
  1 Corinthians 12:25, helping
  Hebrews 10:23–24, exaltation
  2 Timothy 2:15, knowledge
  2 Corinthians 9:7 giving

6. God gave apostles, prophets, evangelists, pastor and teacher to prepare people for service to mature and build.

7. Answer in your own words.

Chapter 9—Answers on Prayer and Quiet Time with God

1. Hebrews 13:15, Offer a sacrifice of praise—the fruit of the lips. Confess His name.
2. James 5: 13–16, Prayers for healing, for forgiveness of sin, and prayers for our troubles.

3. 1st John 1:9, if we confess our sins in prayer and God will forgive us.
James 1:5, pray for wisdom and God will give it to you. Matthew 26:41 Watch and pray that we do not fall into temptation. Colossians 1:9–12 pray that God provides for others. 1 Thessalonians 5:17–18, it is God's will that we pray continually giving thanks.

4. Our minds are more alert in the mornings. We are not bogged down by the days' problems. Giving God the day prepares us spiritually. Although we may choose any time of the day morning seems to be the best.

5. Mark 1:35, early in the morning.

6. Luke 10:38–42, Martha was too busy. She was a believer but was too distracted. Mary wanted to be around and with the Lord. She made the better choice.

7. Distract us with other things. Discourage us by getting us to give up praying. Disqualify us by enticing us to sin and not seeking forgiveness.

8.1 John 3:22, He answers our prayers because we obey His commandments and do Things that please God.

9. Matthew 6:5–6, do not pray showing how religious you are to others. Pray in private unless you are praying with other Christians corporately.

10. Mathew 6:7-8, we should not repeat or merely recite phrases and come to the point.

11. 2 Corinthians 12:8–9, Paul asked God three times but God said His Grace was sufficient.

12. in your own words write out a prayer using Jesus' model.

13. Deuteronomy 9:18–19, For God not to destroy Israel for their sin. 1 Samuel 1:11–12, they mourned the death of Saul and the men of Israel. Luke 4:1, Jesus went to be tempted by the Devil. Jesus started of His ministry.
Luke 2:36–38, she lived in the Temple prayed and worshiped.

14. Isaiah 58:4, to make our voices heard on high. Isaiah 58:5, to humble ourselves before God and seek an attitude of repentance.
Isaiah 58:6, to seek deliverance for ourselves and others. Isaiah 58:7to give to the poor, house the homeless, and clothe the naked. Isaiah 58:8, we will get healing and the Lord will be with you. Isaiah 58:9 the Lord will hear your prayers and answer them. Your relationship will be renewed with God and you will be refreshed in the spirit.

15. Acts 9:34, they were encouraged and strengthened by the Holy Spirit. They had peace and grew in number.

16. Deuteronomy 6:24, Fear the Lord for our good always and for our survival. Jeremiah10:6-7, Fear God because there is none like Him.

17. Proverbs 9:10, Fear of God is the beginning of wisdom, Knowledge, and understanding of God.

18. Psalm 103:11–17, God will love them. Psalm 33:18–19, God will deliver them. Ecclesiastes 8:12-13, God will favor them. Proverbs 14:26–27, God will protect them.

19. Ecclesiastes 12:13, Fear God.

Chapter 10—Answers on False Beliefs

1. Luke 10:18, Jesus saw Satan fall from heaven.
2. Colossians 2:6–10, since we have received Jesus as Lord we should live in Him with thankfulness. We should let no one deceive us with philosophy, human traditions, and principles.

3. Job 1:7, He roams to and fro throughout the earth.
1 Peter 5:8, Be alert, Satan prowls around to see who he can devour.

4. Luke 22: 31–32, Permission from God.

5. Acts 17:11–12, we should double check all you hear and read in Scripture to be true.

6. John 14:6, Jesus said He is the way, the truth and the life. He said no person will be saved to eternal life with the Father without going through Him which means having Him as your savior and Lord. There is no other way or truth that can save.

7. 1st Thessalonians 1:10, God the Father raised Jesus from the dead. Romans 8:11, The Holy Spirit raised Jesus from the dead. John 2:19–21 Jesus raised Himself from the dead.

Chapter 11—Answers on Spiritual Warfare

1. 2 Corinthians 4:4, Satan keeps unbelievers in the dark about the gospel. 1 Thessalonians 2:18, Satan tries to stop the work of God.
2. John 16:11, Satan has been judged. John 12:31, Satan has been cast out of heaven. 2 Corinthians 4:3–6, God has brought forth His Son Jesus; a light to His Glory in this dark world. Mark 3:27, Satan has been bound and tied (limited in what he may do). Colossians 2:15, Satan has been disarmed. Hebrews 2:14–15 Satan has been defeated.

3. John 17:15, Not to take His believers them out of this world but to protect them from the devil.

4. 1 John 5:18, the evil one cannot touch him.

5. 1 John 4: 1–4, every spirit that acknowledges Jesus has come in the flesh. Jesus is inside our hearts and we recognize His truth spoken.

6. 1 Peter 5:8–9, be alert for the enemy is on the prowl to see who he can attack!

7. Matthew 4:1–11, Jesus responds in faith immediately with the right Scripture for the issue (the sword of the Spirit). He does not argue or discuss the matter with the devil. Jesus responded the same way throughout the ordeal.

8. Philippians 4:13, we can do all things through God who strengthens us.

9. James 4:7–8, Submit to God and resist the devil and he will flee from you. Draw near to God and do not sin and confess your sin. Purify your heart (your inner thoughts).

10. Acts 20:27–31, that people moved by Satan would enter the Church to and deceive with false doctrine.

11. John 14:6 Put on Jesus Christ. He is the truth and the way.

12. Jeremiah 23:6, The Lord our righteousness.

13. Romans 5:1–2, we are justified by faith, we have peace with God through Christ, We have Grace to stand by faith, and we rejoice in the hope of the glory of God.

14. Isaiah 26:3, those who trust in the Lord and whose mind is stayed on Him have perfect peace.

15. Proverbs 30:5, God is a shield to those who trust Him. His every word is pure.

16. Colossians 3:1–3, by seeking those things from above. By setting our minds on things above where Christ is, because our lives are hidden with God in Christ.

17. James 4:6–8, oppose the proud for He gives grace to the humble. Submit to God, resist the devil and he will flee. Come near to God and He will come near to you. Purify yourself, do not sin but repent of your sin.

Chapter 12—Answers on Sharing Your Faith

1. Romans 1:16, Paul is not ashamed of the gospel because it is the power of God to save who ever may believe it.

2. Matthew 4:19, He will make His followers Fishers of people (evangelize the lost). We must follow and try to be as close to Him as we can be. We must be filled with the Spirit. Stay in the Word and in prayer so your witness will be in the Spirit and effective.

3. Proverbs 11:30, a wise person wins souls.

4. Hebrews 4:12, The Word of God is living, active, sharper than a two edged sword. It pierces the soul and spirit of man and is able to judge the thoughts and heart.

5. Acts 4:23–31, they prayed for boldness.

6. 2 Timothy 2:24–26, be kind and gentle to those who do not believe, that they may change by your example and the word you give. Always be ready to give the gospel to someone and the hope in you.

7. Write these verses that you should be familiar with out in the space from your Bible.

8. Make a list of those you need to pray for and talk to about Jesus.

Chapter 13—Answers on Living for His Coming

1. Galatians 5: 19–21 The deeds of the flesh are immorality, sensuality, idolatry, sorcery, enmities, strife, jealousy, outbursts of anger, disputes, dissensions, factions, envying, drunkenness, carousing etc.
Ephesians 5:3-4 Immorality, impurity, greed, filthiness, silly talk, coarse jesting.

2. Galatians 5:21 People who practice those things will not inherit the kingdom of God.

3. Self-examination question.

The Narrow Path

For orders, call (909) 627-9288 or visit Livingpathministries.com.

Sources

Barker, Kenneth, Editor, *Study Bible, New International Version*, (NIV), Zondervan Publishing, 1995. *The New Open Bible, Study Edition, New American Standard Bible*, (NASB), Thomas Nelson, Inc., 1990.

Elwell, Walter A. and Buckwalter, Douglas, Editors, *Topical Analysis of the Bible with the New International Version*, Baker Book House Company, 1991.

Elwell, Walter A., *Evangelical Dictionary of Theology*, Baker Book House, 1984.

Emmaus Bible School Staff, *What Christians Believe*, Moody Press Chicago, 1949.

Gosswiller, Richard, *Praying According to the Divine Pattern Prescribed by Our Lord Jesus Christ*, Living in Christ
Ministries, 2006.

Ibid, *Expository Studies in the Epistles of John*, Living in Christ Ministries, 1993.

Ibid, *Winning the Battle in Spiritual Warfare*, Living in Christ Ministries, 2006.

Guralnik, David B., Editor, *Webster's New World Dictionary Second College Edition*, World Publishing, 1968.

Life Application Bible, New Living Translation, (NLT), Tyndale House Publishers Inc., 1996.

MacArthur, John, *John MacArthur Study Bible, New American Standard Bible*, (NASB), Thomas Nelson, 2006.

Ibid, *John MacArthur Study Bible, New King James Version*, (NKJV), Thomas Nelson, 1982.

Manton, Thomas, *A Practical Commentary on the Epistles of James*, Maranatha, ND.

Ogden, Greg, *Discover the Fullness of the Life in Christ for Yourself and Others*, Greg Ogden Discipling Ministries, 1987.

Strong, James, *Strong's Exhaustive Concordance of the Bible*, Hendrickson Publishers.

Vine, W. E., Unger, Merrill F., White, William, *Vine's Expository of Biblical Words*, Thomas Nelson, 1985.